Taste of H

HAPPY HOUR

MORE THAN 100 COCKTAILS, MOCKTAILS, MUNCHIES & MORE

TASTE OF HOME BOOKS • RDA ENTHUSIAST BRANDS, LLC • MILWAUKEE, WI

Taste of Home

© 2018 RDA Enthusiast Brands, LLC
1610 N. 2nd St., Suite 102,
Milwaukee WI 53212

Visit us at **tasteofhome.com** for other
Taste of Home books and products.

International Standard Book Number:
978-1-61765-738-2
Library of Congress Control Number:
2017963396

Cover Photographer: Dan Roberts
Set Stylist: Melissa Franco
Food Stylist: Kathryn Conrad

Pictured on front cover:
Fresh Lime Margaritas, page 68;
Cerveza Margaritas, page 79
Pictured on spine:
Pomegranate Cosmo, page71
Pictured on title page:
Brandy Slush, page 116
Pictured on back cover (from left):
Salmon Party Spread, page 187;
Bloody Maria, page 112
Holiday Rum Balls, page 175

Printed in China.
1 3 5 7 9 10 8 6 4 2

**White Christmas
Sangria,** page 104

GET SOCIAL WITH US

To find a recipe tasteofhome.com
To submit a recipe tasteofhome.com/submit
To find out about other *Taste of Home* **products** shoptasteofhome.com

LIKE US
facebook.com/tasteofhome

TWEET US
twitter.com/tasteofhome

FOLLOW US
@tasteofhome

PIN US
pinterest.com/taste_of_home

TABLE OF CONTENTS

Marinated Mozzarella, page 188
Moscow Mule, page 7

Everything you need for the
Happiest Happy Hours!

It's five o' clock somewhere. Raise a glass and make a toast, because the key to hosting the perfect party is in your hands with *Taste of Home Happy Hour.*

Whether throwing a great big bash, a swanky cocktail party or a traditional holiday get-together, you're bound to impress with the 100+ ideas, shortcuts and recipes found here.

From all-time classics such as martinis to new favorites like Pear Ginger Mojitos, look no further for the perfect sippers.

You'll also find tasty nonalcoholic, or "mocktail," options throughout the book.

A bonus chapter of easy appetizers helps complete any menu, and the luscious Boozy Desserts section features treats calling for ingredients such as bourbon, rum and Irish cream.

Stir up today's cocktails, serve the sort of finger foods guests crave and, most important, enjoy time with friends when you invite everyone over for happy hour!

Texas Salsa,
page 196

**Sparkling
Peach Bellinis,**
page 31

THE ESSENTIAL BAR

A well-stocked bar doesn't need to be extensive: a handful of liquors and mixers, garnishes and tools form a foundation for most of the cocktails in this book. Next, add specialty items based on individual recipes. And always make sure you have ice!

MUST-HAVE LIQUORS
Rum • Bourbon or whiskey • Gin •
Vodka •Tequila • Brandy

BEYOND THE BASICS
Bitters • Orange liqueur (Cointreau or Grand Marnier) • Amaretto • Coffee liqueur (Kahlua) • Irish cream liqueur • Flavored vodkas & rums •Vermouth

FRUIT, VEGGIES & HERBS
Citrus fruits • Seasonal stone fruits and berries • Herbs (mint, rosemary & basil)

MIXERS
Club soda • Tonic water • Colas, ginger ale & lemon-lime soda • Fruit juices • Simple syrup • Grenadine syrup

WINES
White • Red • Rose • Champagne or sparkling white wine • Port

THE TOOL KIT
Cocktail shaker and strainer • Jigger • Muddler • Bottle/wine opener • Peeler • Citrus press • Straws • Cocktail skewers or picks

GLASSES & MORE
Highball (Collins) • Lowball (rocks) • Champagne flute • Martini (cocktail)• Margarita • Wine Glass • Pitcher

HOW TO MAKE SIMPLE SYRUP
Combine 1 cup water and 1 cup sugar in a saucepan over medium-high heat; bring to a boil. Boil for 5 minutes, stirring occasionally. Allow the syrup to cool in the pan, and store in a glass jar in the refrigerator for up to 1 month.

HOW TO MUDDLE A DRINK
Place ingredients such as citrus or herbs in a glass. Add a small amount of sugar or bitters. With a muddler, gently crush and bruise the ingredients until they release their aromas. A wooden spoon handle is a good stand-in if you don't have a muddler.

CLASSIC
COCKTAILS

MOSCOW MULE

Here's an old-time cocktail that was first popular in the 1940s and '50s. It's traditionally served in a copper mug with plenty of ice.

START TO FINISH: 5 MIN.
MAKES: 6 SERVINGS

- 4 **cups ginger beer, chilled**
- ⅔ **cup lime juice**
- 1¼ **cups vodka**
  Ice cubes
  Lemon or lime slices, optional

Combine the ginger beer, lime juice and vodka in a pitcher. Serve over ice. If desired, serve with lemon or lime slices.

LONG ISLAND ICED TEA

Smooth but potent describes this drink. Adjust the tequila to suit your taste: For a bolder flavor, use one ounce; use half an ounce for a more mellow drink.

START TO FINISH: 5 MIN.
MAKES: 1 SERVING

- 1 **to 1¼ cups ice cubes**
- 1 **ounce vodka**
- ½ **to 1 ounce tequila**
- 1 **ounce light rum**
- 1 **ounce sour mix**
- 1 **ounce Triple Sec**
- ½ **ounce cola**

Place ice cubes in a Collins or highball glass. Pour the remaining ingredients into the glass; stir.

NOTES

_____
_____
_____
_____
_____
_____
_____

PINA COLADAS

PREP: 20 MIN. + CHILLING
MAKES: 6 SERVINGS

2¼ cups unsweetened pineapple juice
 1   can (15 ounces) cream of coconut
1½ cups light rum
 5   cups crushed ice
     Pineapple wedges

In a 2-qt. pitcher, combine pineapple juice, cream of coconut and rum. Refrigerate, covered, until chilled. For each serving, add a generous cup of rum mixture and 1 cup ice to a blender. Process, covered, until smooth. Pour into a chilled hurricane or highball glass. Cut a 1-in. slit into tip of a pineapple wedge; slide wedge over rim of glass.

This drink delivers velvety smooth texture and a taste of the tropics. Easy to make, it can be mixed and chilled ahead of time. When ready to serve, just blend for a creamy and delicious beverage.

—LINDA SCHEND KENOSHA, WI

MANHATTAN

This classic New York drink belongs in the hands of whiskey (or bourbon!) drinkers.

START TO FINISH: 5 MIN.
MAKES: 1 SERVING

Ice cubes
2 ounces whiskey
½ ounce sweet vermouth
2 to 3 dashes bitters, optional
Maraschino cherry

Fill a shaker three-fourths full with ice. Add whiskey, vermouth and, if desired, bitters; cover and shake until condensation forms on outside of shaker. Strain into an ice-filled glass. Garnish with a maraschino cherry.

TEQUILA SUNRISE

Everyone loves the pretty sunset layers in this refreshing cocktail. It's like a mini vacation in a glass!

START TO FINISH: 5 MIN.
MAKES: 1 SERVING

1 to 1¼ cups ice cubes
1½ ounces tequila
4½ ounces orange juice
1½ teaspoons grenadine syrup
Orange slice and maraschino cherry, optional

Place ice in a Collins or highball glass. Pour the tequila and orange juice into the glass. Slowly pour grenadine over a bar spoon into the center of the drink. Garnish with an orange slice and a cherry, or as desired.

MOJITO SLUSH

Whether you're splashing poolside or watching the kids inside, this slushy beverage has just the right balance of minty crispness and tart lime. It's sure to tingle your taste buds.
—JESSICA RING CHICAGO, IL

PREP: 30 MIN. + FREEZING
MAKES: 13 SERVINGS (ABOUT 2 QUARTS SLUSH MIX)

- 1 **package (3 ounces) lime gelatin**
- 2 **tablespoons sugar**
- 1 **cup boiling water**
- 1 **cup fresh mint leaves**
- 2 **cans (12 ounces each) frozen limeade concentrate, thawed**
- 2 **cups cold water**
- 2 **cups grapefruit soda**

EACH SERVING
- ⅔ **cup grapefruit soda**
   Lime wedge and/or fresh mint leaves, optional

1. In a small bowl, dissolve gelatin and sugar in boiling water; add mint leaves. Cover and steep for 20 minutes. Press through a sieve; discard mint. Stir in the limeade concentrate, cold water and soda. Pour into a 2½-qt. freezer container. Freeze overnight or until set.
2. For each serving, scoop ⅔ cup slush into a glass. Pour soda into the glass; garnish as desired.

MAKE MINE A
Mocktail

HELPFUL HINT

White Russians are traditionally served without mixing. Once served, guests can either stir the contents or let them blend naturally as they sip.

WHITE RUSSIAN

This creamy coffee-flavored drink is the star at most occasions and perfect for any season. It's equally appropriate before or after dinner.

START TO FINISH: 5 MIN.
MAKES: 1 SERVING

- ½ to ¾ cup ice cubes
- 1½ ounces vodka
- 1½ ounces Kahlua
- 3 ounces heavy whipping cream or milk

Place ice in a rocks glass. Add vodka and Kahlua; top with cream.

BLACK RUSSIAN

Here's a no-fuss beverage that is smooth as silk. A lighter drink and a shorter pour than the related White Russian, it's a great one to start off the evening.

START TO FINISH: 5 MIN.
MAKES: 1 SERVING

- ¾ to 1 cup ice cubes
- 1 ounce vodka
- 1 ounce Kahlua

Place ice in a rocks glass. Pour the vodka and Kahlua into the glass.

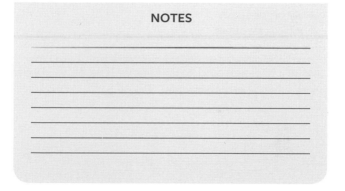

NOTES

DILL BLOODY MARYS

With a nice level of pepper and just enough dill from the pickle, these Bloody Marys are sure to please. Fun garnishes make them like a meal unto themselves!

—**JAY FERKOVICH** GREEN BAY, WI

START TO FINISH: 10 MIN.
MAKES: 2 SERVINGS

- 1½ cups Clamato juice, chilled
- 2 tablespoons dill pickle juice
- 1 tablespoon Worcestershire sauce
- ¼ teaspoon celery salt
- ⅛ to ¼ teaspoon pepper
- ⅛ teaspoon hot pepper sauce
- ¼ cup vodka
  Ice cubes
- 2 celery ribs
- 2 pepperoni-flavored meat snack sticks
- 2 dill pickle spears
- 2 pitted ripe olives

In a small pitcher, combine the first six ingredients. Stir in vodka. Pour into two glasses filled with ice; garnish with celery, snack sticks, pickles and olives.

NOTES

MIMOSA

A standard offering at brunch, mimosas are as pretty as they are tasty. Make sure the champagne you use is extra-dry or dry (not brut), so it doesn't overpower the orange juice.

START TO FINISH: 5 MIN.
MAKES: 1 SERVING

- 2 **ounces champagne or other sparkling wine, chilled**
- ½ **ounce Triple Sec**
- 2 **ounces orange juice**
  Orange slice, optional

Pour champagne into a champagne flute or wine glass. Pour the Triple Sec and orange juice into the glass. Garnish with an orange slice, or as desired.

NOTE *To make a pitcher of mimosas that will serve 12, slowly pour one bottle (750 ml) of chilled champagne into a pitcher. Stir in 3 cups orange juice and ¾ cup Triple Sec.*

MAI TAI

START TO FINISH: 5 MIN.
MAKES: 1 SERVING

1½ to 2 cups ice cubes
2 ounces light rum
¾ ounce Triple Sec
½ ounce lemon juice
1½ teaspoons lime juice
1½ teaspoons amaretto
   Lime slice and twist, optional

1. Fill a shaker three-fourths full with ice. Place the remaining ice in a rocks glass; set aside.
2. Add the rum, Triple Sec, juices and amaretto to the shaker; cover and shake for 10-15 seconds or until condensation forms on outside of shaker. Strain into prepared glass. Garnish with a slice and twist of lime, sliced strawberries or as desired.

This party favorite has been around for quite some time. It's not overly fruity and features a good blend of sweet and sour. For a splash of color, garnish with strawberries and lime.

BRANDY OLD-FASHIONED SWEET

In Wisconsin, this old-fashioned favorite is made with brandy in place of whiskey and soda instead of water for a milder, sweet cocktail.

START TO FINISH: 10 MIN.
MAKES: 1 SERVING

- 1   orange slice
- 1   maraschino cherry
- 1½ ounces maraschino cherry juice
- 1   teaspoon bitters
- ¼ to ⅓ cup ice cubes
- 1½ ounces brandy
- 2   teaspoons water
- 1   teaspoon orange juice
- 3   ounces lemon-lime soda

In a rocks glass, muddle orange slice, cherry, cherry juice and bitters. Add ice. Pour in brandy, water, orange juice and soda.

SCOTCH OLD-FASHIONED *In a rocks glass, muddle 1 orange slice, 1 maraschino cherry, ½ teaspoon sugar and 3-4 dashes bitters. Add ice. Add 2 ounces of Scotch and a splash of club soda.*

GIMLET

In this classic sweet-tart cocktail, a touch of confectioners' sugar smooths out an otherwise puckery drink. Bring out your inner bartender—try mixing it with vodka instead of gin, or straining it into a chilled cocktail glass and serving it neat.

START TO FINISH: 5 MIN.
MAKES: 1 SERVING

-     Ice cubes
- 2   ounces gin
- 1   ounce lime juice
- 1   teaspoon confectioners' sugar
-     Lime slices

Fill a shaker three-fourths full with ice. Add gin, lime juice and confectioners' sugar; cover and shake for 10-15 seconds or until condensation forms on outside of shaker. Strain into an ice-filled glass. Garnish with lime.

NOTE *You may also strain the gimlet into a chilled cocktail glass and serve without additional ice.*

VODKA GIMLET *Substitute vodka for the gin.*

TOM COLLINS

This cocktail has been popular for a long time, but the origin of the name is still up for debate. Some think it was named after a sweet gin called Old Tom, while others believe the drink was named for the bartender who invented it.

START TO FINISH: 5 MIN.
MAKES: 1 SERVING

1½ to 2 cups ice cubes, divided
2 ounces gin
1½ ounces sour mix
½ cup club soda, chilled
    Orange slice and maraschino cherry

1. Fill a shaker three-fourths full with ice. Place remaining ice in a Collins or highball glass; set aside.

2. Add the gin and sour mix to shaker; cover and shake for 10-15 seconds or until condensation forms on outside of shaker. Strain into prepared glass. Pour club soda into glass. Garnish with an orange slice and a maraschino cherry.

HELPFUL HINT

To add a bigger burst of fresh mint flavor (and aroma!) muddle a few mint leaves with sugar in the glass before adding the drink ingredients.

MINT JULEP

It wouldn't be Kentucky Derby day without Mint Juleps!
If you're hosting kids as well as adults, you can make a
nonalcoholic version, too, that tastes just as great.

PREP: 30 MIN. + CHILLING
MAKES: 10 SERVINGS (2½ CUPS SYRUP)

MINT SYRUP
- 2 **cups sugar**
- 2 **cups water**
- 2 **cups loosely packed chopped fresh mint**

EACH SERVING
- ½ **to ¾ cup crushed ice**
- ½ **to 1 ounce bourbon**
- **Mint sprig**

1. For syrup, combine the sugar, water and chopped
mint in a large saucepan. Bring to a boil over medium
heat; cook until sugar is dissolved, stirring occasionally.
Remove from the heat; cool to room temperature.

2. Line a mesh strainer with a double layer of cheesecloth
or a coffee filter. Strain syrup; discard mint. Cover and
refrigerate syrup for at least 2 hours or until chilled.

3. For each serving, place ice in a metal julep cup or a rocks
glass. Pour ¼ cup mint syrup and bourbon into the glass;
stir until mixture is well-chilled. Garnish with mint sprig.

MOCK MINT JULEP *Prepare mint syrup as directed.
After straining, add ½ cup lemon juice. Cover and
refrigerate for at least 2 hours or until chilled. For each
serving, combine ½ cup club soda and ¼ cup mint syrup
in a glass filled with crushed ice. Garnish with mint.*

MARTINI

It's not a true cocktail party without a martini on the menu. The choice of gin or vodka is up to you, but either way, this queen-of-the-cocktail-hour drink comes shaken, not stirred.

START TO FINISH: 5 MIN.
MAKES: 1 SERVING

> Ice cubes
> 3 ounces gin or vodka
> ½ ounce dry vermouth
> Pimiento-stuffed olives

Fill a shaker three-fourths full with ice. Add gin and vermouth; cover and shake until condensation forms on outside of shaker. Strain into a chilled cocktail glass. Garnish with an olive.

NOTE *This recipe makes a dry martini. Use less vermouth for an extra-dry martini; use more for a wet martini. You may also serve the martini over ice in a rocks glass.*

CHOCOLATE MARTINI *Omit dry vermouth and olives. Use vodka (not gin) but reduce amount to 2 ounces; add 2 ounces crème de cacao or chocolate liqueur. Shake until condensation forms on outside of shaker. Strain into a chilled cocktail glass; garnish with chocolate shavings.*

CHAMPAGNE
SPARKLERS

SPARKLING PEACH BELLINIS

Serve this elegant champagne beverage at a special brunch. Your guests will love the subtle peach flavor.

PREP: 35 MIN. + COOLING
MAKES: 12 SERVINGS

- 3 **medium peaches, halved**
- 1 **tablespoon honey**
- 1 **can (11.3 ounces) peach nectar, chilled**
- 2 **bottles (750 milliliters each) champagne or sparkling grape juice, chilled**

1. Preheat oven to 375°. Line a baking sheet with a large piece of heavy-duty foil (about 18x12 in.). Place peach halves, cut sides up, on foil; drizzle with honey. Fold foil over peaches and seal.
2. Bake for 25-30 minutes or until tender. Cool completely; remove and discard peels. In a food processor, process peaches until smooth.
3. Transfer peach puree to a pitcher. Add nectar and 1 bottle of champagne; stir until combined. Pour into 12 champagne flutes or wine glasses; top with the remaining champagne. Serve immediately.

CHAMPAGNE FRUIT PUNCH

START TO FINISH: 10 MIN.
MAKES: 16 SERVINGS (¾ CUP EACH)

- 2 cups fresh or frozen raspberries
- 1 can (12 ounces) frozen orange juice concentrate, thawed
- 1 can (12 ounces) frozen cherry pomegranate juice concentrate, thawed
- 1 can (6 ounces) unsweetened pineapple juice, chilled
- 1 medium lemon, thinly sliced
- 1 bottle (1 liter) club soda, chilled
- 1 bottle (750 milliliters) champagne or sparkling white grape juice, chilled

In a punch bowl, combine the first five ingredients. Slowly stir in club soda and champagne. Serve immediately.

Toast the happy couple at your next bridal shower with a fun and fruity drink! It's the perfect refreshment.

—KELLY TRAN SALEM, OR

MANMOSA

Here's a guy-friendly adaptation of the sweet and fruity mimosa that still has that classic mimosa fizz.

—MIKE DIETIKER ELBURN, IL

START TO FINISH: 5 MIN.
MAKES: 2 SERVINGS

- 1 **bottle (12 ounces) beer, chilled**
- 1 **cup orange juice**
- 2 **ounces Triple Sec**
  Mint sprigs, optional

Divide beer between two tall glasses. Add ½ cup orange juice and 1 ounce Triple Sec to each glass. Garnish with a sprig of mint, or as desired.

NOTES

CITRUS CHAMPAGNE SPARKLER

This festive beverage is perfect for toasting the bride at her shower.

—SHARON TIPTON CASSELBERRY, FL

START TO FINISH: 10 MIN.
MAKES: 11 SERVINGS

- 1¼ cups orange juice
- ⅓ cup orange liqueur
- ⅓ cup brandy
- ¼ cup sugar
- ¼ cup lemon juice
- ¼ cup unsweetened pineapple juice
- 6 cups champagne, chilled

In a pitcher, combine the first six ingredients, stirring until the sugar is dissolved. Pour ¼ cup into individual champagne flutes or wine glasses. Top with champagne.

RASPBERRY FIZZ

Adults will especially enjoy this pretty pink drink. It has a mild raspberry taste and isn't overly sweet.

START TO FINISH: 5 MIN.
MAKES: 1 SERVING

- 2 ounces ruby red grapefruit juice
- ½ to 1 ounce raspberry flavoring syrup
- ½ to ¾ cup ice cubes
- 6 ounces club soda, chilled

In a mixing glass or tumbler, combine grapefruit juice and syrup. Place ice in a highball glass; add juice mixture. Top with club soda.
NOTE *This recipe was tested with Torani brand syrup, which can be found in the coffee section of the grocery store.*

NOTES

MAKE MINE A
Mocktail

MIMOSA FLOATS

START TO FINISH: 5 MIN.
MAKES: 4 SERVINGS

1½ cups champagne, chilled
½ cup no-pulp orange juice
1 cup vanilla ice cream
Shaved dark chocolate, optional

Pour 6 tablespoons champagne and 2 tablespoons orange juice into a 6-ounce champagne flute. Stir in ¼ cup vanilla ice cream; if desired, top with chocolate shavings. Repeat with remaining ingredients.

Everyone needs a little treat at brunch! I wanted to kick things up a notch, so I added a scoop of ice cream to my mimosas.

—**AMY LENTS** GRAND FORKS, ND

APPLE CIDER SMASH

A smash is a fruity and chilled cocktail—very refreshing! It's a great use for those apples you bought from the orchard plus some sparkling cider.

—MOFFAT FRAZIER NEW YORK, NY

START TO FINISH: 20 MIN.
MAKES: 16 SERVINGS

- 2 **cups finely chopped Gala or other red apples (about 2 small)**
- 2 **cups finely chopped Granny Smith apples (about 2 small)**
- 2½ **cups bourbon**
- ⅔ **cup apple brandy**
- 4 **teaspoons lemon juice**
  Ice cubes
- 5⅓ **cups sparkling apple cider, chilled**

1. In a bowl, toss apples to combine. In a small pitcher, mix bourbon, brandy and lemon juice.

2. To serve, fill each of 16 rocks glasses halfway with ice. To each, add ¼ cup apple mixture and 3 tablespoons bourbon mixture; top with ⅓ cup cider.

HELPFUL HINT

If you're mixing these to order at a party, stir a bit of lemon juice into the bowl with the chopped apples; it will keep them from turning brown.

CRANBERRY ORANGE MIMOSAS

Mimosas are such an elegant addition to Sunday brunch. My recipe uses tart cranberries to balance the sweetness of the champagne and orange juice.
—**SHANNON STEPHENS** LAKE IN THE HILLS, IL

PREP: 10 MIN.
MAKES: 12 SERVINGS

- 2 **cups fresh or frozen cranberries**
- 3 **cups orange juice, divided**
- 2 **tablespoons lemon juice**
- 3 **bottles (750 milliliters each) champagne, chilled**
  Fresh mint leaves, optional

1. Place cranberries and 1 cup orange juice in a blender; cover and process until pureed, stopping as needed to scrape down the sides with a rubber spatula. Add lemon juice and the remaining orange juice; cover and process until blended.

2. Pour ⅓ cup cranberry mixture into individual champagne flutes or wine glasses. Top each with ¾ cup champagne; serve with mint if desired.

NOTES

_____

_____

_____

_____

_____

_____

_____

BUBBLY CHAMPAGNE PUNCH

This punch was served at my wedding, and to this day it continues to be the elegant drink we ladle up for special events.

—ANITA GEOGHAGAN WOODSTOCK, GA

PREP: 10 MIN. + FREEZING
MAKES: 16 SERVINGS (¾ CUP)

 3 orange slices, halved
   Fresh or frozen cranberries
2½ cups unsweetened pineapple juice
1½ cups ginger ale
 2 bottles (750 milliliters each) brut champagne, chilled
 1 bottle (375 milliliters) sweet white wine, chilled
 1 can (12 ounces) frozen lemonade concentrate, thawed

1. Line the bottom of a 6-cup ring mold with orange slices and cranberries. Combine pineapple juice and ginger ale; pour over the fruit. Freeze until solid.

2. Just before serving, unmold the ice ring into a punch bowl. Gently stir in remaining ingredients.

RED CARPET-TINI

Bubbly champagne gets a fruity punch courtesy of pomegranate juice and raspberry and orange liqueur.

START TO FINISH: 5 MIN.
MAKES: 1 SERVING

> Ice cubes
> 1 ounce raspberry liqueur
> ½ ounce orange liqueur
> ½ ounce pomegranate juice
> 3 fresh raspberries
> ½ cup champagne, chilled

1. Fill a mixing glass or tumbler one-third full with ice. Add the raspberry liqueur, orange liqueur and pomegranate juice; stir until condensation forms on the outside of the glass.
2. Place raspberries in a chilled champagne flute or cocktail glass; strain liqueur mixture into glass. Top with champagne.

HELPFUL HINT

Try fresh pomegranate seeds as an alternative garnish in the Red Carpet-Tini. The seeds will sink, so you'll get a different visual effect.

BELLA BASIL RASPBERRY TEA

Give iced tea a grown-up twist. The fresh basil lends bright flavor and the raspberries, beautiful color, and you'll love the fun fizz and the make-ahead convenience.

—**LAURIE BOCK** LYNDEN, WA

PREP: 45 MIN. + CHILLING
MAKES: 6 SERVINGS

> 3 cups fresh raspberries
> 1 cup sugar
> 1 cup packed fresh basil leaves, coarsely chopped
> ¼ cup lime juice
> 2 individual black tea bags
> 1 bottle (750 milliliters) sparkling rose wine, chilled
> Ice cubes
> Fresh raspberries, optional

1. In a large saucepan, combine the raspberries, sugar, basil and lime juice. Mash the berries. Cook over medium heat for 7 minutes or until berries release juices.
2. Remove from heat; add tea bags. Cover and steep for 20 minutes. Strain, discarding tea bags and raspberry seeds. Transfer tea to a 2-qt. pitcher. Cover and refrigerate until serving.
3. Just before serving, slowly add wine. Serve over ice. If desired, top with raspberries.
NOTE *To make a nonalcoholic version, use 1 bottle (1 liter) carbonated water instead of the sparkling rose wine.*

ORANGE-APRICOT MIMOSA PUNCH

START TO FINISH: 10 MIN.
MAKES: 20 SERVINGS (¾ CUP EACH)

- 1 **cup orange liqueur**
- ½ **cup sugar**
- 4 **cups orange-tangerine juice, chilled**
- 2 **cups apricot nectar, chilled**
- 1 **can (6 ounces) frozen orange juice concentrate, thawed**
- 1 **bottle (1 liter) club soda, chilled**
- 1 **bottle (750 milliliters) champagne or other sparkling wine, chilled**
  Thinly sliced oranges

In a punch bowl, combine liqueur and sugar until sugar is dissolved. Stir in orange-tangerine juice, apricot nectar and orange juice concentrate. Just before serving, stir in soda and champagne. Top with orange slices.

For parties, I triple this recipe and chill the punch with an orange-studded ice ring.

—**KATHY MCKAY** ACWORTH, GA

HELPFUL HINT

It's not worth splurging on a high-priced champagne for a fruity cocktail. Choose a modestly priced bottle of champagne or sparkling wine, such as a prosecco.

STRAWBERRY MIMOSAS

Here's a tasty twist on the classic mimosa. To make this refreshing drink friendly for kids or mamas-to-be, substitute lemon-lime soda or ginger ale for the champagne.
—**KELLY MAXWELL** PLAINFIELD, IL

START TO FINISH: 15 MIN.
MAKES: 12 SERVINGS (1 CUP EACH)

- 7 **cups sliced fresh strawberries (about 2 quarts)**
- 3 **cups orange juice**
- 4 **cups champagne, chilled**
  Fresh strawberries and orange slices, optional

1. Place half of the strawberries and orange juice in a blender; cover and process until smooth. Press through a fine mesh strainer. Repeat with remaining strawberries and orange juice.

2. Pour a scant ⅔ cup strawberry mixture into each champagne flute or wine glass. Top with about ⅓ cup champagne. If desired, garnish with a strawberry, orange slice or both.

NOTES

CHAMPAGNE COCKTAIL

This amber drink is a champagne twist on the traditional old-fashioned. Try it with extra-dry champagne.

START TO FINISH: 5 MIN.
MAKES: 1 SERVING

- **1 sugar cube or ½ teaspoon sugar**
- **6 dashes bitters**
- **½ ounce brandy**
- **½ cup champagne, chilled**
  Fresh rosemary sprig and fresh or frozen cranberries, optional

Place sugar in a champagne flute or cocktail glass; sprinkle with bitters. Add brandy; top with champagne. If desired, top with a sprig of rosemary and 2-3 cranberries.

MARTINIS & MARGARITAS

PERFECT LEMON MARTINI

Time to relax with a refreshing cocktail! The combination of tart lemon and sweet liqueur will tingle your taste buds.

—MARILEE ANKER CHATSWORTH, CA

START TO FINISH: 5 MIN.
MAKES: 1 SERVING

- 1 **lemon slice**
- **Sugar**
- **Ice cubes**
- 2 **ounces vodka**
- 1½ **ounces limoncello**
- ½ **ounce lemon juice**

1. Using the lemon slice, moisten the rim of a chilled cocktail glass; set lemon aside. Sprinkle sugar on a plate; hold glass upside down and dip rim into sugar. Discard the remaining sugar on the plate.

2. Fill a shaker three-fourths full with ice. Add vodka, limoncello and lemon juice; cover and shake for 10-15 seconds or until condensation forms on outside of shaker. Strain into prepared glass. Garnish with lemon slice if desired.

COFFEE & CREAM MARTINI

With Kahlua, Irish cream liqueur and chocolate syrup, this martini is almost like a dessert. It's an after-dinner drink that's easy to mix.

—CLARA COULSON MINNEY WASHINGTON COURT HOUSE, OH

START TO FINISH: 10 MIN.
MAKES: 1 SERVING

- 2 **tablespoons coarse sugar**
- 1 **teaspoon finely ground coffee**
   Ice cubes
- 1½ **ounces vodka**
- 1½ **ounces Kahlua**
- 1½ **ounces Irish cream liqueur**
   Chocolate syrup

1. Sprinkle sugar and coffee on a plate. Moisten the rim of a cocktail glass with water; hold glass upside down and dip rim into sugar mixture.
2. Fill a mixing glass or tumbler three-fourths full with ice. Add the vodka, Kahlua and liqueur; stir until condensation forms on outside of glass.
3. Drizzle chocolate syrup on the inside of prepared martini glass. Strain vodka mixture into glass.

NOTES

FROZEN LEMON-BERRY MARGARITAS

I like to cool down with this absolutely fantastic margarita. It's slightly icy, thick and perfect for when you need a break.
—JULIE HIEGGELKE GRAYSLAKE, IL

START TO FINISH: 15 MIN.
MAKES: 4 SERVINGS

- 4 **lime wedges**
- 2 **tablespoons coarse sugar**
- ⅔ **cup thawed lemonade concentrate**
- 1 **cup frozen unsweetened raspberries**
- 2 **cups ice cubes**
- 2 **packages (10 ounces each) frozen sweetened sliced strawberries, thawed**
- ½ **cup frozen blueberries**
- 1 **tablespoon sugar**

1. Using lime wedges, moisten the rims of four margarita or cocktail glasses. Set aside limes for garnish. Sprinkle coarse sugar on a plate; hold each glass upside down and dip rim into sugar. Set aside. Discard the remaining sugar on plate.
2. In a blender, combine lemonade concentrate and raspberries; cover and process until blended. Press mixture through a fine sieve; discard seeds. Return raspberry mixture to blender; add the ice, strawberries, blueberries and sugar. Cover and process until smooth.
3. Pour into the prepared glasses. Garnish with reserved limes if desired.

KUMQUAT MARGARITAS

These golden margaritas bring a bit of sunshine to a winter table. Eye-catching kumquats are the secret ingredient. Check your produce section; they're worth it for the exotic touch!

START TO FINISH: 20 MIN.
MAKES: 4 SERVINGS

- 4 lime wedges
- 3 tablespoons kosher salt
- ¾ cup tequila
- 1 pint kumquats (about 30)
- 3 tablespoons lime juice
- 3 cups crushed ice
- ⅓ cup sugar

1. Using lime wedges, moisten the rims of four margarita or cocktail glasses. Sprinkle salt on a plate; dip rims in salt. Set glasses aside.
2. Place tequila in a blender. Rinse kumquats; cut in half and remove seeds. Add to blender; cover and process until pureed. Strain, discarding skins and pulp.
3. Return puree to blender. Add lime juice, ice and sugar; cover and process until blended. Pour into the prepared glasses.

ORANGE RAZZLETINI

Raspberry-flavored rum and orange juice? We gave it a try and loved it! Try this spirited combination with a splash of Triple Sec at your next holiday event.

START TO FINISH: 5 MIN.
MAKES: 2 SERVINGS

- Ice cubes
- ½ cup orange juice
- 2 ounces raspberry-flavored rum
- ½ ounce Triple Sec
- Orange peel or slices and fresh raspberries, optional

1. Fill a mixing glass or tumbler three-fourths full with ice. Add orange juice, rum and Triple Sec; stir until condensation forms on outside of glass.
2. Strain into two chilled cocktail glasses. Garnish with orange peel or orange slices and raspberries if desired.

RUBY ROSE PALOMA

START TO FINISH: 10 MIN.
MAKES: 2 SERVINGS

- 1 **cup ruby red grapefruit juice**
- 4 **ounces mezcal or tequila**
- 1 **tablespoon fresh lime juice**
- 1½ **teaspoons rose water**
- 1 **tablespoon kosher salt**
- 1 **teaspoon coarse sugar**
- ½ **cup grapefruit soda**
   Grapefruit slices

1. In a small pitcher, combine the first four ingredients.
2. Mix salt and sugar on a plate. Moisten the rims of two cocktail glasses with water. Hold each glass upside down and dip moistened rim into salt mixture. Discard remaining salt mixture.
3. To serve, fill glasses with ice. Add half the grapefruit juice mixture to each; top with grapefruit soda and grapefruit slices.

Rose water adds a delicate touch to citrusy grapefruit and lime. If you can't find rose water in your area, you can order it online.

—**GINA NISTICO** MILWAUKEE, WI

ORANGE & COFFEE MARTINI

With its pretty jeweled color and complementary orange-coffee flavor, this impressive martini lends an elegant, upscale feel to any occasion.

START TO FINISH: 5 MIN.
MAKES: 1 SERVING

2 tablespoons coarse sugar and orange zest
  Ice cubes
2 ounces strong brewed coffee, cooled
1 ounce vodka
½ ounce orange liqueur
½ ounce hazelnut liqueur
  Orange slice, optional

1. Mix sugar and orange zest on a plate. Moisten the rims of a cocktail glass. Hold the glass upside down and dip rim into sugar mixture. Set glass aside.
2. Fill a mixing glass or tumbler three-fourths full with ice. Add remaining ingredients; stir until condensation forms on the outside of glass. Strain into prepared cocktail glass.

NOTES

HELPFUL HINT

You can make a large batch of martini mix in advance by combining the coffee, vodka and liqueurs. Refrigerate until time to serve, then mix ½ cup of mix into the tumbler for each cocktail.

CRANBERRY-JALAPENO MARTINI

I describe this cocktail as slightly tart, a little sassy and completely delicious. I make a big batch when I'm hosting a party because it disappears quickly. Garnish with fresh mint and cranberries for an extra-special touch.

—KELLI HAETINGER VIRGINIA BEACH, VA

PREP: 30 MIN + CHILLING
MAKES: 16 SERVINGS

- 1 cup turbinado (washed raw) sugar
- 1½ cups cranberry juice, divided
- ½ cup fresh or frozen cranberries
- ½ teaspoon chopped seeded jalapeno pepper
  Ice cubes
- 6 cups vodka
  Fresh mint leaves and additional cranberries, optional

1. In a large saucepan, combine the sugar, ½ cup cranberry juice, cranberries and jalapeno. Bring to a boil. Reduce heat; simmer, uncovered, for 3 minutes or until sugar is dissolved. Remove from the heat. Cover and let stand for 20 minutes.

2. Strain, discarding cranberries and jalapeno. Cover and refrigerate syrup for at least 2 hours or until chilled.

3. For each serving, fill a mixing glass or tumbler three-fourths full with ice. Add 3 ounces vodka, 1 tablespoon cranberry juice and 1 tablespoon cranberry syrup; stir until condensation forms on outside of glass. Strain into a chilled cocktail glass. Repeat. Garnish with mint and cranberries if desired.

NOTE *Wear disposable gloves when cutting hot peppers; the oils can burn exposed skin. Avoid touching your face.*

FRESH LIME MARGARITAS

This basic margarita recipe is easy to modify to your tastes.
Try it frozen or with strawberries.

START TO FINISH: 15 MIN.
MAKES: 4 SERVINGS

- 4 **lime wedges**
- 1 **tablespoon kosher salt**
- ½ **cup tequila**
- ¼ **cup Triple Sec**
- ¼ **cup lime juice**
- ¼ **cup lemon juice**
- 2 **tablespoons superfine sugar**
- 1⅓ **cups crushed ice**

1. Moisten the rims of four margarita or cocktail glasses with lime wedges. Sprinkle salt on a plate; dip rims in salt.
2. In a pitcher, combine tequila, Triple Sec, lime juice, lemon juice and sugar; stir until the sugar is dissolved. Serve in the prepared glasses over crushed ice.

FROZEN LIME MARGARITAS *Reduce lemon and lime juices to 2 tablespoons each. Increase the superfine sugar to ¼ cup and the crushed ice to 4 cups. Add ¾ cup limeade concentrate. Prepare glasses as directed. In a blender, combine the tequila, Triple Sec, lime juice, lemon juice, limeade concentrate, superfine sugar and crushed ice; cover and process until smooth. Yield: 5 cups.*

FROZEN STRAWBERRY MARGARITAS *Follow directions for Frozen Lime Margaritas, except reduce crushed ice to 2 cups and add 2 cups frozen unsweetened strawberries. Yield: 4 cups.*

HELPFUL HINT

The classic margarita glass is a wide bowl with a stem, but you can use a tumbler or cocktail glass. Go for a larger diameter to get the full benefit of the salted rim.

POMEGRANATE COSMO

Every soirée needs a signature drink. Colored sugar dresses up this simple cosmo that lets you enjoy a cozy evening with friends and still shake things up.

START TO FINISH: 10 MIN.
MAKES: 1 SERVING

- 1 tablespoon coarse red decorating sugar
- ¾ to 1 cup ice cubes
- 1½ ounces lemon-lime soda
- 1½ ounces pomegranate liqueur or cranberry-pomegranate juice
- 1 ounce X-Rated fusion liqueur
- ½ ounce Triple Sec
- 1 ounce cranberry-pomegranate juice
  Lemon peel strip, optional

1. Sprinkle red sugar on a plate. Moisten rim of a cocktail glass with water; dip rim in sugar to coat. Set aside.
2. Fill a shaker three-fourths full with ice. Add the soda, liqueurs and juice; cover and shake 10-15 seconds or until condensation forms on outside of shaker. Strain into prepared glass. If desired, garnish with lemon peel.

NOTES

_____
_____
_____
_____
_____
_____
_____

APPLE MARTINI

START TO FINISH: 5 MIN.
MAKES: 1 SERVING

Ice cubes
2 ounces vodka
1½ ounces sour apple liqueur
1½ teaspoons lemon juice
Green apple slice, or apple peel strip

Fill a shaker three-fourths full with ice. Add the vodka, apple liqueur and lemon juice. Cover and shake for 10-15 seconds or until condensation forms on outside of shaker. Strain into a chilled cocktail glass. Garnish with a slice of green apple or a strip of apple peel, as desired.

You'll feel like a movie star when you sip this fancy apple martini! Impress your guests by garnishing each pretty drink with a green apple slice or a delicate strip of apple peel.

BLUE LAGOON MARGARITAS

A special toast to anyone who mixes up a batch of these margaritas for a summer soirée. Guests will swoon over the citrusy sweet tang and electrifying shade of blue.

—WILLIE DEWAARD CORALVILLE, IA

START TO FINISH: 15 MIN.
MAKES: 4 SERVINGS

- 4 lime slices
- 3 tablespoons coarse sugar
- ½ cup chilled lemon-lime soda
- ½ cup tequila
- ½ cup blue curacao
- ⅓ cup partially thawed frozen limeade concentrate
- 2 cups ice cubes

1. Using lime slices, moisten rims of four margarita or cocktail glasses. Set aside lime slices. Sprinkle sugar on a plate; hold each glass upside down and dip rim into sugar. Set aside. Discard remaining sugar on plate.

2. In a blender, combine the remaining ingredients; cover and process until blended. Pour into prepared glasses. Garnish with reserved lime slices.

BUTTERSCOTCH MARTINIS

For guests who want to sip a little something sweet, we dress up our vodka martinis with butterscotch schnapps and chocolate.

—CLARA COULSON MINNEY
WASHINGTON COURT HOUSE, OH

START TO FINISH: 10 MIN.
MAKES: 2 SERVINGS

- Ice cubes
- 2 ounces clear creme de cacao
- 2 ounces creme de cacao
- 1½ ounces vodka
- 1½ ounces butterscotch schnapps liqueur
- 6 semisweet chocolate chips

1. Fill a shaker three-fourths full with ice. Add the creme de cacao, vodka and schnapps. Cover and shake for 10-15 seconds or until condensation forms on outside of the shaker.

2. Divide chocolate chips between two chilled cocktail glasses; strain butterscotch mixture over chips.

CHOCOLATE ESPRESSO MARTINI

After-dinner drinks and dessert come together delightfully in this coffee-flavored cocktail that's sure to perk up chocolate and java lovers.

START TO FINISH: 5 MIN.
MAKES: 1 SERVING

Ice cubes
2½ ounces chocolate liqueur
½ ounce brewed espresso
½ ounce vanilla-flavored vodka
Coarse sugar

1. Sprinkle sugar on a plate. Moisten the rim of a chilled cocktail glass with water; hold glass upside down and dip rim into sugar. Set aside.
2. Fill a mixing glass or tumbler three-fourths full with ice. Add chocolate liqueur, espresso and vodka; stir until condensation forms on outside of glass. Strain vodka mixture into glass.

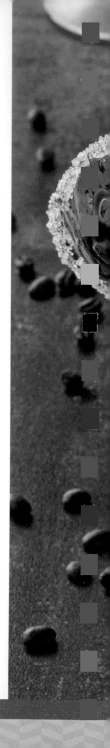

HELPFUL HINT

For extra flair, drizzle 1 teaspoon of chocolate syrup on the inside of each glass before pouring in the martini. Other possible garnishes include cocoa powder mixed with the sugar, or chocolate-covered espresso beans.

CERVEZA MARGARITAS

One sip of this refreshing drink and you'll picture sand, sea and blue skies that stretch for miles. It's like a vacation in a glass, and you can mix it up in moments.

—CHRISTINA PITTMAN PARKVILLE, MO

START TO FINISH: 10 MIN.
MAKES: 5 SERVINGS

- 1 **can (12 ounces) lemon-lime soda, chilled**
- 1 **bottle (12 ounces) beer**
- 1 **can (12 ounces) frozen limeade concentrate, thawed**
- ¾ **cup tequila**
  Lemon and lime slices and kosher salt, optional
  Crushed ice

In a pitcher, combine all the liquid ingredients. If desired, moisten rims of margarita or cocktail glasses with lime slices. Sprinkle salt on a plate; dip rims in salt. Serve in prepared glasses over crushed ice with additional lemon and lime slices.

NOTES

PUMPKIN PIE MARTINIS

My girlfriends start asking me to make these in the fall and continue to request them throughout the holidays. Dessert martinis are always a fun way to end a holiday meal.

—CATHLEEN BUSHMAN GENEVA, IL

START TO FINISH: 5 MIN.
MAKES: 2 SERVINGS

- 1 **vanilla wafer, crushed, optional**
  Ice cubes
- 2 **ounces vanilla-flavored vodka**
- 2 **ounces milk**
- 2 **ounces heavy whipping cream**
- 1 **ounce simple syrup**
- 1 **ounce hazelnut liqueur**
- ⅛ **teaspoon pumpkin pie spice**
  Dash ground cinnamon

1. For a cookie-crumb rim, moisten the rims of two chilled cocktail glasses with water. Place cookie crumbs on a plate; dip rims in crumbs. Set aside.

2. Fill a mixing glass three-fourths full with ice. Add the remaining ingredients; stir until condensation forms on the outside of the glass. Strain into the two prepared cocktail glasses.

NOTE *You may substitute 1 ounce pumpkin flavoring syrup for the simple syrup and pumpkin pie spice. Look for flavoring syrup in the coffee section.*

TO MAKE AHEAD *Prepare a martini mix of vodka, milk, cream, syrup and liqueur. Shake mix before using; pour 1 cup into the mixing glass for each batch of drinks. Add spices and proceed as directed.*

SUPER SANGRIAS &
·WINE COCKTAILS·

SANGRIA WINE

My citrus-spiked wine is always the life of the party, whether I serve it on a hot summer evening or a chilly winter day. The bubbles give it some extra pop.

—COLLEEN STURMA MILWAUKEE, WI

START TO FINISH: 10 MIN.
MAKES: 10 SERVINGS

- **1 bottle (750 milliliters) dry red wine**
- **1 cup lemon-flavored rum**
- **2 cans (12 ounces each) lemon-lime soda, chilled**
- **2 medium lemons, sliced**
- **2 medium limes, sliced**
- **!ce cubes**

In a pitcher, combine the wine, rum and soda; add lemon and lime slices. Serve over ice.

SPRING STRAWBERRY SANGRIA

PREP: 10 MIN. + CHILLING
MAKES: 10 SERVINGS (ABOUT 2 QUARTS)

- 4 **cups dry white wine, chilled**
- ½ **pound fresh strawberries, hulled and sliced**
- ¼ **cup sugar**
- 2 **cups club soda, chilled**
- 2 **cups champagne**

1. In a pitcher, combine wine, strawberries and sugar. Refrigerate at least 1 hour.
2. Just before serving, stir in club soda and champagne.

> Wine-infused strawberries make a lovely addition to this sparkling beverage. I love serving it in springtime to celebrate the season.
>
> **—GINA QUARTERMAINE** ALEXANDRIA, VA

TOPSY-TURVY SANGRIA

I got this recipe from a friend a few years ago. It's perfect for relaxed get-togethers. It tastes best when you make it the night before and let the flavors steep. But be careful—it goes down easy!

—TRACY FIELD BREMERTON, WA

START TO FINISH: 10 MIN.
MAKES: 10 SERVINGS (¾ CUP EACH)

- 1 **bottle (750 milliliters) merlot**
- 1 **cup sugar**
- 1 **cup orange liqueur**
- ½ **to 1 cup brandy**
- 3 **cups cold lemon-lime soda**
- 1 **cup sliced fresh strawberries**
- 1 **medium orange, sliced**
- 1 **medium lemon, sliced**
- 1 **medium peach, sliced**
  Ice cubes

In a pitcher, stir first four ingredients until sugar is dissolved. Stir in soda and fruit. Serve over ice.

NOTES

SPICY APRICOT SANGRIA

This sweet-tart fruit punch is scented with cinnamon, allspice and cloves, which makes it a fantastic beverage for winter and fall. If you like use, 1 medium red-skinned apple and 1 medium green-skinned apple for even more color.

—TINA BELLOWS RACINE, WISCONSIN

PREP: 25 MIN. + CHILLING
MAKES: 7 SERVINGS

- 3 **cinnamon sticks (3 inches)**
- 10 **whole allspice**
- 10 **whole cloves**
- 6 **cups apricot nectar**
- 1 **cup water**
- ½ **cup lemon juice**
- 2 **cups ginger beer, chilled**
- 1 **large apple, cubed**
- 1 **large pear, cubed**
- 1 **medium orange, sliced**
- 1 **medium lemon, sliced**
  Fresh mint leaves, optional

1. Place the cinnamon, allspice and cloves on a double thickness of cheesecloth; bring up corners of cloth and tie with string to form a bag.

2. Place the apricot nectar, water, lemon juice and spice bag in a large saucepan. Bring to a boil. Remove from the heat; cover and steep for 5 minutes. Transfer to a pitcher. Cover and refrigerate at least 3 hours. Discard spice bag.

3. Just before serving, add the ginger beer, fruits and, if desired, mint leaves.

MAKE MINE A
Mocktail

HELPFUL HINT

You can make this sangria
a pleasing pink by using
regular red cranberry
juice instead of white.

MIXED BERRY SANGRIA

This light, tasty beverage is so refreshing. I like to serve it with spoons so everyone can enjoy the fresh berries once the sangria is gone.
—LINDA CIFUENTES MAHOMET, IL

PREP: 10 MIN. + CHILLING
MAKES: 10 SERVINGS (¾ CUP EACH)

- 1 **bottle (750 milliliters) sparkling white wine**
- 2½ **cups white cranberry juice**
- ⅔ **cup light or coconut rum**
- ⅓ **cup each fresh blackberries, blueberries and raspberries**
- ⅓ **cup chopped fresh strawberries**
  Ice cubes

In a large pitcher, mix wine, juice and rum; add fruit. Refrigerate at least 2 hours; serve over ice.

NOTES

HOT SPICED WINE

PREP: 10 MIN. • **COOK:** 4 HOURS
MAKES: 8 SERVINGS

- 2 cinnamon sticks (3 inches)
- 3 whole cloves
- 3 medium tart apples, peeled and sliced
- ½ cup sugar
- 1 teaspoon lemon juice
- 2 bottles (750 milliliters each) dry red wine

1. Place cinnamon sticks and cloves on a double thickness of cheesecloth. Gather the corners of the cloth to enclose spices; tie securely with string. Place in a 3-qt. slow cooker.
2. Add the remaining ingredients. Cook, covered, on low until the flavors are blended, 4-5 hours. Discard spice bag. Serve warm.

My friends, family and I enjoy this spiced wine during cold-winter gatherings. This warm drink will be especially pleasing to people who enjoy dry red wines.
—**NOEL LICKENFELT** BOLIVAR, PA

GRILLED PEACH &
PINEAPPLE SANGRIA

Grill up fresh peaches and pineapple slathered in cinnamon butter and use them to make a refreshing summer sangria. I also like to add slices of grilled lemon and lime to drop in the glass for a citrusy boost of flavor.

—HEATHER KING FROSTBURG, MD

PREP: 25 MIN. + CHILLING
MAKES: 8 SERVINGS

- 1 **bottle (750 milliliters) sauvignon blanc or other white wine**
- 2 **cups lemonade**
- ½ **cup orange liqueur**
- 1 **tablespoon butter, melted**
- 1 **tablespoon sugar**
- 1 **teaspoon ground cinnamon**
- 3 **medium peeled peaches, pitted and halved**
- ¼ **fresh pineapple, peeled and cut into 4 slices**

1. Make sangria by combining wine, lemonade and liqueur. Refrigerate.

2. Meanwhile, in a small bowl, combine melted butter, sugar and cinnamon. Mix well. Brush butter mixture over cut side of peaches and all over pineapple slices. Grill fruit, covered, on a greased rack over medium direct heat 4-5 minutes. Turn peaches and pineapple. Grill 4-5 minutes more. Remove from grill.

3. Cut each peach half into five or six slices and each pineapple slice into five or six pieces. Add three-fourths of fruit to sangria, reserving the remainder. Refrigerate at least 2 hours.

4. Before serving, thread several pieces of the reserved fruit onto appetizer skewers. Pour sangria over ice; serve with fruit skewers.

CRANBERRY-ORANGE SANGRIA

For sangria with a little sass, we chill this drink overnight to make it even more fruity. It helps with party prep, too.

—MARIA REGAKIS SAUGUS, MA

PREP: 15 MIN. + CHILLING
MAKES: 10 SERVINGS

- 1 medium orange, halved and thinly sliced
- 1 medium apple, quartered and thinly sliced
- ½ cup fresh or frozen cranberries
- 1 bottle (32 ounces) cranberry juice
- 1 bottle (750 ml) zinfandel or other fruity red wine
- 1 cup simple syrup
- ½ cup orange liqueur
  Ice cubes
  Additional thinly sliced oranges, apples and fresh cranberries, optional

In a large pitcher, combine the first seven ingredients; refrigerate overnight. Serve over ice; garnish with oranges, apples and cranberries if desired.

CRANBERRY-LIME SANGRIA

Tart, light and fruity, this party-worthy sangria is a hit at any time of the year.

—KATY JOOSTEN LITTLE CHUTE, WI

START TO FINISH: 20 MIN.
MAKES: 13 SERVINGS (¾ CUP EACH)

- 2 **cups water**
- 1 **cup fresh or frozen cranberries, thawed**
- 1 **bottle (750 milliliters) white wine, chilled**
- ¾ **cup frozen limeade concentrate, thawed**
- 1 **each medium orange, lime and apple, peeled and diced**
- 1 **bottle (1 liter) lemon-lime soda, chilled**

1. In a small saucepan, combine water and cranberries. Cook over medium heat until the berries pop, about 5 minutes. Drain and discard liquid; set cranberries aside.
2. In a pitcher, combine the wine and limeade concentrate. Stir in the diced fruit and reserved cranberries; add the soda. Serve over ice.

NOTES

PEACH WINE COOLERS

PREP: 15 MIN. + CHILLING
MAKES: 9 SERVINGS

  2 **cups frozen unsweetened sliced peaches, thawed**
  ½ **cup brandy**
  ⅓ **cup honey**
  ½ **lemon, very thinly sliced**
  1 **bottle (750 milliliters) dry white wine**
1½ **cups carbonated water, chilled**
     Ice cubes

1. In a 2-qt. pitcher, combine the peach slices, brandy, honey and lemon slices; stir in wine. Refrigerate for 2-4 hours or until chilled.
2. Just before serving, stir in carbonated water. Serve over ice.

The fantastic flavors of honey, wine and brandy come through to make a special drink for your fiesta. It's like sunshine in a glass!

—ANNIE HENDRICKS BURBANK, CA

HELPFUL HINT

When adding sugar to a cocktail mix, use superfine sugar to allow it to dissolve more easily. As an alternative, use an equivalent amount of simple syrup (see page 5).

SANGRIA BLANCO

Using white instead of red wine makes my version of sangria a bit lighter, yet with the same wonderful sweetness. Frozen fruit allows me to serve this refreshing sipper any time of year.

—SHARON TIPTON CASSELBERRY, FL

START TO FINISH: 15 MIN.
MAKES: 6 SERVINGS

- ¼ **cup sugar**
- ¼ **cup brandy**
- 1 **cup sliced peeled fresh or frozen peaches, thawed**
- 1 **cup sliced fresh or frozen sliced strawberries, thawed**
- 1 **medium lemon, sliced**
- 1 **medium lime, sliced**
- 1 **bottle (750 milliliters) dry white wine, chilled**
- 1 **can (12 ounces) lemon-lime soda, chilled**
  Ice cubes

In a pitcher, mix sugar and brandy until sugar is dissolved. Add the remaining ingredients; stir gently to combine. Serve over ice.

WHITE CHRISTMAS SANGRIA

This fruity sparkling sangria is alcohol free, so everyone in your family can feel like a VIP.

START TO FINISH: 10 MIN.
MAKES: 21 SERVINGS (3¾ QUARTS)

- 6 **cups white cranberry juice, chilled**
- ¾ **cup thawed lemonade concentrate**
- 3 **bottles (25.40 ounces each) sparkling grape juice**
  Pomegranate seeds and sliced grapefruit, oranges and kiwi, optional

Combine cranberry juice and lemonade concentrate in a punch bowl or pitcher; pour in sparkling grape juice. If desired, add pomegranate seeds and sliced fruit. Serve immediately.

NOTES

_____

_____

_____

_____

_____

_____

_____

MAKE MINE A *Mocktail*

SPRING &
· SUMMER SIPPERS ·

BLACK-EYED SUSAN

The Kentucky Derby has the mint julep; the Preakness has the black-eyed Susan. The drink is a sunny mix of vodka, rum, and pineapple and orange juices to toast your special events.

START TO FINISH: 5 MIN.
MAKES: 1 SERVING

- ½ to ¾ cup crushed ice
- 1 ounce vodka
- 1 ounce light rum
- ½ ounce Triple Sec
- 2 ounces unsweetened pineapple juice
- 2 ounces orange juice
  Lime slice and pitted sweet dark cherry

Place desired amount of ice in a rocks glass. Pour vodka, rum, Triple Sec and juices into glass. Stir; serve with a lime slice and cherry.

PEAR GINGER MOJITO

Pear-flavored vodka, ginger beer and cinnamon syrup turn a traditional mojito into a refresher for any season. Add a lime slice or wedge to each glass as a garnish, if you'd like.

START TO FINISH: 10 MIN.
MAKES: 2 SERVINGS

- 1 medium pear, peeled and thinly sliced
- 4 teaspoons maple syrup
- 2 lime wedges
- 1 cup ginger beer, chilled
- 4 ounces pear-flavored vodka
- 2 tablespoons cinnamon flavoring syrup or 2 dashes ground allspice
- 2 dashes bitters
- 2 cups ice cubes
  Lime slices or wedges, optional

In each of two cocktail glasses, muddle half of the pear slices with 2 teaspoons maple syrup. Squeeze one lime wedge into each glass. Divide the remaining ingredients between both glasses; stir. Garnish with lime slices or wedges if desired.

PASSION FRUIT HURRICANES

This version of the famous New Orleans beverage uses real fruit juice. They're named hurricanes because each sip packs a punch!

START TO FINISH: 10 MIN.
MAKES: 6 SERVINGS

- 2 cups passion fruit juice
- 1 cup plus 2 tablespoons sugar
- ¾ cup lime juice
- ¾ cup light rum
- ¾ cup dark rum
- 3 tablespoons grenadine syrup
- 6 to 8 cups ice cubes
  Orange slices, starfruit slices and maraschino cherries

1. In a pitcher, combine passion fruit juice, sugar, lime juice, rum and grenadine; stir until the sugar is dissolved.
2. Pour into hurricane or highball glasses filled with ice. Serve with orange slices, starfruit slices and maraschino cherries.

MAKE MINE A
Mocktail

ROSEMARY LEMONADE

PREP: 10 MIN. • **COOK:** 15 MIN. + CHILLING
MAKES: 8 SERVINGS (1 CUP EACH)

  2 **cups water**
  2 **fresh rosemary sprigs**
  ½ **cup sugar**
  ½ **cup honey**
1¼ **cups fresh lemon juice**
  6 **cups cold water**
     Ice cubes
     Additional lemon slices and fresh rosemary
        sprigs, optional

1. In a small saucepan, bring 2 cups water to a boil; add rosemary sprigs. Reduce heat; simmer, covered, 10 minutes.
2. Remove and discard rosemary. Stir in sugar and honey until dissolved. Transfer to a pitcher; refrigerate 15 minutes.
3. Add lemon juice; stir in cold water. Serve over ice. If desired, top with additional lemon slices and rosemary sprigs for garnish.

A friend suggested I add a sprig of rosemary to lemonade. The herb makes the drink taste fresh and light.
—**DIXIE GRAHAM** RANCHO CUCAMONGA, CA

BLOODY MARIA

Tequila, lime and jalapenos give the brunch classic a fresh Mexican twist.

START TO FINISH: 10 MIN.
MAKES: 6 SERVINGS

- 4 **cups tomato juice, chilled**
- 8 **ounces (1 cup) tequila**
- ½ **cup lime juice**
- 4 **to 8 teaspoons juice from pickled jalapeno slices**
- 1 **tablespoon Worcestershire sauce**
- 2 **to 4 teaspoons hot pepper sauce**
- ¼ **teaspoon celery salt**
- ¼ **teaspoon pepper**
- 2 **teaspoons prepared horseradish, optional**
  Pickled jalapeno slices
  Pepper jack cheese, cubed
  Lime wedges

Mix the first eight ingredients in a 2-qt. pitcher; stir in horseradish if desired. Pour over ice; serve with jalapenos, cheese cubes and lime wedges.

NOTES

THIN MINT MILK SHAKE

START TO FINISH: 5 MIN.
MAKES: 2 SERVINGS

- 3 tablespoons creme de menthe or
  3 tablespoons 2% milk plus a dash
  of peppermint extract
- 1¼ to 1½ cups vanilla ice cream
- 7 Girl Scout Thin Mint cookies
  Green food coloring, optional

Place all ingredients in a blender in the order listed; cover and process until blended. Serve immediately.

These creamy milk shakes go over big with kids as well as adults—just be sure to save the creme de menthe for the grownups!

—SHAUNA SEVER SAN FRANCISCO, CA

BRANDY SLUSH

This citrusy slush is a Midwestern party go-to. For variety, swap in other spirits for regular brandy, like a berry vodka or blackberry brandy.

PREP: 15 MIN. + FREEZING
MAKES: 21 SERVINGS
(ABOUT 4 QUARTS SLUSH MIX)

- **4 individual green or black tea bags**
- **9 cups water, divided**
- **2 cups brandy**
- **1 can (12 ounces) frozen lemonade concentrate, thawed**
- **1 can (12 ounces) frozen orange juice concentrate, thawed**

EACH SERVING
- **¼ cup lemon-lime soda, chilled**
- **Lime wedge, optional**

1. Place tea bags in a small bowl. Bring 2 cups water to a boil; pour over tea bags. Cover and steep for 5 minutes. Discard tea bags. Transfer tea to a large pitcher; stir in the brandy, lemonade concentrate, juice concentrate and the remaining water. Pour into a 4-qt. freezer container. Freeze overnight or until set.
2. For each serving, scoop ¾ cup slush into a rocks glass. Pour lemon-lime soda into the glass; if desired, serve with lime wedge.

OLD FASHIONED SLUSH *Combine 9 cups water, 2 cups bourbon, 2 cans orange juice concentrate and 2 tablespoons bitters. Pour into a 4-qt. freezer container. Freeze overnight or until set. For each serving, scoop ¾ cup slush into a rocks glass; top with lemon-lime soda.*

CRANBERRY BOG SLUSH *Combine 9 cups water, 2 cups vodka, 1 can cranberry juice and 1 can limeade concentrate. Pour into a 4-qt. freezer container. Freeze overnight or until set. For each serving, scoop ¾ cup slush into a rocks glass; top with ginger ale.*

SOUTHERN SWEET TEA SLUSH *Combine 9 cups water, 2 cups sweet tea vodka, 2 cans lemonade concentrate. Pour into a 4-qt. freezer container. Freeze overnight or until set. For each serving, scoop ¾ cup slush into a rocks glass; top with lemon-lime soda.*

NEGRONI SLUSH *Combine 9 cups water, 1½ cups gin, ½ cup Campari, 1 can limeade, 1 can cranberry concentrate and 2 tablespoons of sweet vermouth. Pour into a 4-qt. freezer container. Freeze overnight or until set. For each serving, scoop ¾ cup slush into a rocks glass; top with lemon-lime soda.*

BLUEBERRY THIRST QUENCHER

I first enjoyed this cocktail at a Kentucky Derby day party and fell in love with it. With its beautiful color and zesty flavor, it's a festive surprise for a summer picnic or party.

—BELINDA J GIBSON DRY RIDGE, KY

START TO FINISH: 5 MIN.
MAKES: 9 SERVINGS

- 6 **cups chilled blueberry juice cocktail**
- 3 **cups chilled lemon-lime soda**
- 9 **ounces blueberry-flavored vodka, chilled**
  Crushed ice
- 1 **cup fresh blueberries**
  Sliced peeled mango, optional

In a large pitcher, combine the juice, soda and vodka. Serve over ice; garnish with blueberries and, if desired, mango slices.

NOTES

SPIKED ORANGE REFRESHER

My two-tone drink always impresses party guests. You can use another citrus fruit in place of oranges if you like, and delete the rum if you want a no-alcohol version.
—**MARYBETH MANK** MESQUITE, TX

PREP: 15 MIN. • **COOK:** 15 MIN. + COOLING
MAKES: 10 SERVINGS

- 3 medium oranges
- 1½ cups turbinado (washed raw) sugar
- 1½ cups water
- 1 cup fresh mint leaves
- 8 slices fresh gingerroot
  Crushed ice
- 5 ounces spiced rum
- 1 bottle (1 liter) club soda, chilled

1. Using a vegetable peeler, remove the colored layer of peel from oranges in strips, leaving the white pith behind. Cut oranges crosswise in half; squeeze juice from oranges.

2. In a small saucepan, combine sugar, water and orange juice; bring to a boil. Stir in mint, ginger and orange peel; return to a boil. Reduce heat; simmer, uncovered, 10 minutes. Cool syrup mixture completely.

3. Strain syrup, discarding solids. To serve, fill 10 highball glasses halfway with ice. Add 2 ounces syrup and ½ ounce rum to each glass; top with soda.

AGUA DE JAMAICA

This is an iced tea made from hibiscus—tart and deep red like cranberry juice—and livened by rum. For a no-alcohol version, just leave out the rum.

—ADAN FRANCO MILWAUKEE, WI

PREP: 15 MIN. + CHILLING
MAKES: 6 SERVINGS

- 1 **cup dried hibiscus flowers or 6 hibiscus tea bags**
- 5 **cups water, divided**
- 1½ **teaspoons grated lime peel**
- ½ **cup sugar**
- 1 **cup rum**
  Mint sprigs, optional

1. Rinse the flowers in cold water. In a large saucepan, combine 3 cups water, flowers (or tea bags) and lime peel. Bring to a boil. Reduce heat; simmer, uncovered, 10 minutes.

2. Remove from heat; let stand 15 minutes. Strain mixture, discarding flowers and lime peel; transfer to a large bowl. Add sugar and remaining water, stirring until sugar is dissolved. Stir in rum. Refrigerate until cold. Add mint sprigs to garnish, if desired.

PINEAPPLE COLADA SHAKE

This frothy shake with refreshing coconut and pineapple flavors is sinfully delicious! With a cool, creamy texture, it begs to be your poolside companion.
—**MELISSA JELINEK** APPLE VALLEY, MN

START TO FINISH: 5 MIN.
MAKES: 1 SERVING

¼ **cup coconut-flavored rum**
½ **cup vanilla ice cream**
½ **cup canned crushed pineapple**
  Ground cinnamon
  Pineapple wedge and
    maraschino cherry

Place the rum, ice cream and pineapple in a blender. Cover and process for 30 seconds or until blended. Transfer to a chilled glass. Sprinkle with cinnamon. Garnish with pineapple and a cherry.

HELPFUL HINT

You can make this shake with fresh pineapple, but it won't be quite as sweet. If you like, add 1-2 tablespoons of simple syrup with the pineapple.

STRAWBERRY-BASIL COCKTAIL

Fresh strawberries and tender basil blend in this refreshing cocktail that isn't overly sweet. It's our family's favorite.
—**MARY MARLOWE LEVERETTE**
COLUMBIA, SC

START TO FINISH: 5 MIN.
MAKES: 1 SERVING

3 **fresh strawberries, thinly sliced**
1 **teaspoon minced fresh basil**
¾ **to 1 cup ice cubes**
2 **ounces vodka**
½ **ounce club soda**
1 **teaspoon simple syrup**
1 **teaspoon cranberry juice**
  Pinch pepper
  Fresh basil leaf, optional

In a shaker, muddle strawberries and basil. Fill shaker three-fourths full with ice. Add the remaining ingredients; cover and shake for 10-15 seconds or until condensation forms on outside of shaker. Strain into a chilled cocktail glass. Add a fresh basil leaf as garnish, if desired.

TIPSY ICED COFFEE

PREP: 10 MIN. + FREEZING
MAKES: 8 SERVINGS

4 **cups strong brewed coffee**
½ **cup amaretto**
¼ **cup plus 3 tablespoons sugar, divided**
⅔ **cup heavy whipping cream**

1. In a large bowl, whisk coffee, amaretto and ¼ cup sugar. Let cool to room temperature.
2. Transfer to an 8-in. square dish. Freeze 1 hour. Stir with a fork. Freeze 2-3 hours longer or until completely frozen, stirring every 30 minutes.
3. Meanwhile, in a small bowl, beat cream until it begins to thicken. Add remaining sugar; beat until stiff peaks form. Cover and refrigerate until serving.
4. To serve, stir mixture with a fork; spoon into glasses. Top with whipped cream. Serve immediately.

My family loves this frozen coffee with amaretto and whipped cream. Serve it at brunch or as an after-dinner treat.
—SONYA LABBE WEST HOLLYWOOD, CA

NEW ENGLAND ICED TEA

While growing up in Massachusetts, I spent summers with my family at our cottage. The clambakes on the beach always included these cocktails—a regional variation on the classic Long Island iced tea— for the adults.

—ANN LIEBERGEN BROOKFIELD, WI

START TO FINISH: 10 MIN.
MAKES: 1 SERVING

- 2 tablespoons sugar
- 1 ounce vodka
- 1 ounce light rum
- 1 ounce gin
- 1 ounce Triple Sec
- 1 ounce lime juice
- 1 ounce tequila
- 1 to 1½ cups ice cubes
- 2 ounces cranberry juice
  Lemon slice, optional

1. In a mixing glass or tumbler, combine the sugar, vodka, rum, gin, Triple Sec, lime juice and tequila; stir until sugar is dissolved.
2. Place ice in a highball glass; pour in the sugar mixture. Top with cranberry juice. Garnish iced tea with lemon slice if desired.

PEACHY KEEN DAIQUIRIS

You won't mind breaking out the blender for these frosty fruit drinks— they're a breeze to whip up with thawed frozen peaches. A dash of grenadine gives the tangy, golden concoction a splash of vibrant color.

—JOAN ANTONEN ARLINGTON, SD

START TO FINISH: 10 MIN.
MAKES: 3 SERVINGS

- 2½ cups ice cubes
- 3 medium peaches, peeled and sliced
- ¾ cup thawed frozen limeade concentrate
- ¼ cup orange juice
- 2 tablespoons confectioners' sugar
- ½ cup rum
  Grenadine syrup, optional

In a blender, combine the ice, peaches, limeade concentrate, orange juice, confectioners' sugar and rum; cover and process for 30 seconds or until smooth. Pour into chilled glasses; add grenadine if desired. Serve immediately.

HOP, SKIP AND GO

Pink lemonade gives this pretty drink a touch of sweetness. Made in the blender and poured into tall slender glasses, it has a frothy, fun look.

START TO FINISH: 10 MIN.
MAKES: 4 SERVINGS

- ¾ cup thawed pink lemonade concentrate
- 1 bottle (12 ounces) beer
- 3 ounces vodka or rum
- 1 cup ice cubes
  Maraschino cherries

In a blender, combine all ingredients. Cover and process until smooth (mixture will be foamy). Pour into hurricane or cocktail glasses. Garnish with maraschino cherries or as desired.

NOTE *If you don't want a frothy head on this drink, combine the lemonade concentrate, vodka and beer in a pitcher. Serve over ice in rocks glasses.*

NOTES

APRICOT BRANDY SLUSH

While we were spending the summer in New Mexico, we tasted this refreshing golden colored tea enhanced with something borrowed from the cocktail world: apricot brandy.

—SHIRLEY MILLER WILLIAMSPORT, PA

PREP: 15 MIN. + FREEZING
MAKES: 8 SERVINGS (6½ CUPS SLUSH MIX)

- 4½ cups water, divided
- 2 tea bags
- 1 cup sugar
- 1 cup apricot brandy
- ¾ cup thawed orange juice concentrate
- ¾ cup thawed lemonade concentrate

EACH SERVING
- ¼ cup lemon-lime soda

1. In a large saucepan, bring 1 cup water to a boil; remove from heat. Add tea bags; steep, covered, 3-5 minutes according to taste. Discard tea bags. Stir in sugar until dissolved. Cool.
2. Stir in apricot brandy, juice concentrates and remaining water. Transfer to a 2-qt. freezer container. Freeze, covered, 6 hours or overnight.
3. For each serving, scoop ¾ cup slush into a rocks glass. Pour soda into glass. Serve immediately.

WINTER & HOLIDAY WARMERS

SWEET KAHLUA COFFEE

Want to perk up your java? With Kahlua, creme de cacao and a dollop of whipped cream, this chocolaty coffee makes the perfect after-dinner treat at Christmas or anytime. It stays warm in the slow cooker.

—RUTH GRUCHOW YORBA LINDA, CA

PREP: 10 MIN. • **COOK:** 3 HOURS
MAKES: 8 SERVINGS (2¼ QUARTS)

- 2 **quarts hot water**
- ½ **cup Kahlua (coffee liqueur)**
- ¼ **cup creme de cacao**
- 3 **tablespoons instant coffee granules**
- 2 **cups heavy whipping cream**
- ¼ **cup sugar**
- 1 **teaspoon vanilla extract**
- 2 **tablespoons grated semisweet chocolate**

1. In a 4-qt. slow cooker, mix water, Kahlua, creme de cacao and coffee granules. Cook, covered, on low for 3-4 hours or until heated through.
2. In a large bowl, beat cream until it begins to thicken. Add the sugar and vanilla; beat until soft peaks form. Serve warm coffee with whipped cream and grated chocolate.

RASPBERRY TRUFFLE COCKTAIL

This adults-only hot chocolate is a decadent addition to any holiday gathering. You can make it with almond milk or dairy products—it's delicious either way.

—MELANIE MILHORAT NEW YORK, NY

START TO FINISH: 10 MIN.
MAKES: 1 SERVING

- 1 **cup chocolate almond milk or 2% chocolate milk**
- 1 **ounce vodka**
- ½ **ounce raspberry liqueur**
- ¼ **cup cold vanilla almond milk or fat-free milk**
  Baking cocoa, optional

1. Place the chocolate almond milk in a small saucepan; heat through. Add vodka and raspberry liqueur; transfer to a mug.

2. Pour vanilla almond milk into a small bowl. With a frother, blend until foamy. Gently spoon foam into mug. Sprinkle with cocoa if desired.

NOTES

MULLED WINE

With a delightful blend of spices and warmed to perfection, this mulled wine is soothing and satisfying. Chilling the wine mixture overnight allows the flavors to blend, so don't make sure you don't omit this essential step.

PREP: 15 MIN. • **COOK:** 30 MIN. + CHILLING
MAKES: 5 SERVINGS

- 1 **bottle (750 milliliters) fruity red wine**
- 1 **cup brandy**
- 1 **cup sugar**
- 1 **medium orange, sliced**
- 1 **medium lemon, sliced**
- ⅛ **teaspoon ground nutmeg**
- 2 **cinnamon sticks (3 inches)**
- ½ **teaspoon whole allspice**
- ½ **teaspoon aniseed**
- ½ **teaspoon whole peppercorns**
- 3 **whole cloves**
  Optional garnishes: orange slices, star anise and additional cinnamon sticks

1. In a large saucepan, combine the first six ingredients. Place the remaining spices on a double thickness of cheesecloth. Gather corners of the cloth to enclose spices; tie securely with string. Place in pan.

2. Bring to a boil, stirring occasionally. Reduce heat; simmer gently, covered, 20 minutes. Transfer to a covered container to cool slightly. Refrigerate, covered, overnight.

3. Strain wine mixture into a large saucepan, discarding the fruit and spice bag; reheat. Serve warm. Garnish as desired with fruit and spices.

NOTE *This recipe was tested with Rioja wine. Merlot would also work well.*

CRANBERRY POMEGRANATE MARGARITAS

I came up with this beverage for a festive twist on the traditional margarita. It's a hit at holiday celebrations, and looks beautiful with sugar crystals on glass rims.
—**MINDIE HILTON** SUSANVILLE, CA

START TO FINISH: 5 MIN.
MAKES: 12 SERVINGS

- 4½ **cups lemon-lime soda, chilled**
- 1½ **cups tequila**
- 1½ **cups cranberry juice, chilled**
- 1½ **cups pomegranate juice, chilled**
     Pomegranate seeds and frozen cranberries, optional

1. Sprinkle sugar on a plate. Moisten the rim of each glass with water, then hold upside down and dip the rim into sugar mixture. Set glasses in refrigerator to chill.

2. In a pitcher, combine soda, tequila and juices. Serve in chilled glasses. Garnish with pomegranate seeds and cranberries if desired.

NOTES

HOLIDAY PEPPERMINT MOCHA

Making this for a group on a snowy night doesn't take any more time than it takes to make it for one. This mocha's also good with a coffee liqueur instead of peppermint. Trust me, I've tried it and liked it—several times!

—LAUREN BRIEN-WOOSTER SOUTH LAKE TAHOE, CA

START TO FINISH: 10 MIN.
MAKES: 8 SERVINGS

- 4 **cups 2% milk**
- 8 **packets instant hot cocoa mix**
- 1½ **cups brewed espresso or double-strength dark roast coffee**
- ¾ **cup peppermint schnapps liqueur or 1 teaspoon peppermint extract plus ¾ cup additional brewed espresso**
  Whipped cream, optional

1. In a large saucepan, heat milk over medium heat until bubbles form around sides of pan. Add the cocoa mix; whisk until blended. Add espresso and heat through.
2. Remove from heat; stir in liqueur. If desired, serve with whipped cream.

HOT APPLE PIE DRINK

A perfect holiday drink for adults, this is simple and fun to make.

START TO FINISH: 20 MIN.
MAKES: 2 SERVINGS

- 2 **cups unsweetened apple juice**
- 4 **teaspoons brown sugar**
- 2 **teaspoons lemon juice**
- ¼ **teaspoon ground cinnamon**
  Dash ground cloves
  Dash ground nutmeg
- 1½ **ounces orange liqueur**
- 1½ **ounces brandy**
  Sweetened whipped cream and additional ground nutmeg, optional

In a small saucepan, heat the first six ingredients until the sugar is dissolved. Remove from the heat; stir in orange liqueur and brandy. Pour into mugs; garnish with whipped cream and additional nutmeg if desired.

HELPFUL HINT

Orange liqueur is any sweetened alcoholic beverage to which orange flavor is added. The most common types are Triple Sec and curacao. The most widely available brands are Grand Marnier (Triple Sec blended with cognac) and Cointreau (straight Triple Sec).

POINSETTIA

START TO FINISH: 5 MIN.
MAKES: 1 SERVING

1 **ounce cranberry juice**
½ **ounce Triple Sec**
4 **ounces chilled champagne or other sparkling wine**
3 **fresh cranberries**

Pour cranberry juice into a champagne flute or wine glass. Add Triple Sec. Top with champagne. Garnish with fresh cranberries or as desired.

NOTE *To make a batch (6 servings), slowly pour one bottle (750 ml) chilled champagne into a pitcher. Stir in ¾ cup cranberry juice and 3 ounces Triple Sec if desired.*

Mixing festive red cranberry juice, Triple Sec and champagne creates a fun cocktail for Christmas parties, a New Year's Eve bash or any get-together during the fall and winter seasons. Garnish with a few fresh berries and enjoy.

MAKE MINE A
Mocktail

VANILLA CITRUS CIDER

My mom used to make cider for the holidays, so I based my citrusy-vanilla variation on her recipe. I think it hits the spot! The longer the cider simmers, the stronger the flavors will be.
—**KRISTIN WEGLARZ** BREMERTON, WA

PREP: 10 MIN. • **COOK:** 70 MIN.
MAKES: 10 SERVINGS

- 8 **cups apple cider or juice**
- ¼ **cup packed brown sugar**
- ¼ **cup thawed orange juice concentrate**
- ⅛ **teaspoon salt**
- 3 **cinnamon sticks (3 inches)**
- 1 **teaspoon whole cloves**
- ¼ **teaspoon vanilla extract**
  Orange slices, optional

1. In a large saucepan, combine apple cider, brown sugar, orange juice concentrate and salt. Place cinnamon sticks and cloves on a double thickness of cheesecloth. Gather corners of cloth to enclose seasonings; tie securely with a string. Add to pan.

2. Bring to a boil. Reduce heat; simmer, covered, 1 hour to allow flavors to blend. Discard the spice bag. Stir in vanilla. If desired, serve with orange slices.

NOTES

MIDNIGHT COCKTAILS

This variation on a mojito uses blackberry spreadable fruit, which gives it a deep purple color and a bit of sweetness in every sip. It's the perfect translation of a summertime sipper into one ideal for winter—especially when made with brandy!

PREP: 15 MIN. + CHILLING
MAKES: 2 SERVINGS

- ⅓ **cup seedless blackberry spreadable fruit**
- 2 **tablespoons water**
- ¼ **cup fresh mint leaves**
- 3 **tablespoons lime juice**
- ⅓ **cup brandy or rum**
- 1 **cup club soda**
  Mint sprigs or lime twist, optional

1. In a small saucepan, combine spreadable fruit and water. Cook and stir over medium heat until smooth; transfer to a small bowl. Refrigerate until chilled.
2. In a small pitcher, muddle mint leaves and lime juice. Add blackberry syrup and brandy. Divide between two cocktail glasses. Stir in club soda; garnish as desired with mint sprigs or a twist of lime.

NOTES

HOLIDAY MIMOSA

START TO FINISH: 5 MIN.
MAKES: 1 SERVING

- 1 **tablespoon red coarse sugar**
- ½ **ounce raspberry liqueur**
- 2 **ounces ruby red grapefruit juice**
- 2 **ounces champagne**
  Grapefruit twist, optional

1. Sprinkle sugar on a plate. Moisten the rim of a champagne flute with water; hold glass upside down and dip rim into sugar.

2. Pour the raspberry liqueur and grapefruit juice into the glass; top with champagne. Garnish with a grapefruit twist, if desired.

NOTE *To make a batch (12 servings), slowly pour one bottle (750 ml) chilled champagne into a pitcher. Stir in 3 cups red grapefruit juice and ¾ cup raspberry liqueur.*

Add a splash of color to your brunch table with this lovely rosy mimosa. It has a fantastic sweet-tart taste.

—JESSIE SARRAZIN LIVINGSTON, MT

FIRESIDE GLOGG

An aromatic blend of spices flavors this superb wine-based, traditional Scandinavian beverage served during the holidays. Always heated, its sweet, fruity taste will warm you to your toes.

—**SUE BROWN** WEST BEND, WI

PREP: 45 MIN. • **COOK:** 20 MIN.
MAKES: 8 SERVINGS

- 4 **cups port wine or apple cider, divided**
- 3 **cups fresh or frozen cranberries, thawed**
- ¼ **cup packed brown sugar**
- 4 **orange peel strips (3 inches)**
- 3 **cinnamon sticks (3 inches)**
- 5 **slices fresh peeled gingerroot**
- 5 **cardamom pods**
- 5 **whole cloves**
- 4 **cups apple cider or juice**
- ½ **cup blanched almonds**
- ½ **cup raisins**

1. In a large saucepan, combine 3 cups wine, cranberries, brown sugar, orange peel, cinnamon, ginger, cardamom and cloves. Cook over medium heat until berries pop, about 15 minutes. Mash slightly and cook 10 minutes longer.
2. Strain and discard pulp, orange peel and spices. Return mixture to pan; stir in cider, almonds, raisins and remaining wine. Bring to a boil. Reduce heat; simmer, uncovered, for 15 minutes.

MAPLE BRANDY PUNCH

Reminiscent of an old-fashioned brandy punch, this smooth, maple-infused beverage adds extra pizzazz to holiday dinner parties and other special occasions.

PREP: 20 MIN. + COOLING
MAKES: 20 SERVINGS

- 1⅓ **cups maple syrup**
- 2 **cups apple brandy**
- 2 **cups Cognac**
- 2 **cups spiced rum**
- ¼ **cup lemon juice**
- 2 **teaspoons bitters**
- 2 **bottles (1 liter each) carbonated water, chilled**
  Ice cubes
  Thin apple slices and lemon twists

1. Place syrup in a small saucepan. Bring to a boil. Reduce heat; simmer, uncovered, for 5 minutes. Remove from the heat and set aside to cool.
2. Combine the brandy, Cognac, rum, lemon juice and bitters in a punch bowl; stir in maple reduction. Add the carbonated water. Serve over ice with thin apple slices and lemon twists.

CREAMY IRISH COFFEE

START TO FINISH: 10 MIN.
MAKES: 4 SERVINGS

3 **cups hot strong brewed coffee**
4 **ounces Irish cream liqueur**
   Sweetened whipped cream,
      optional
   Chocolate shavings, optional

Divide coffee and liqueur among four
mugs; stir. If desired, top with whipped
cream and chocolate shavings.

> My maternal grandmother
> never drank more than a glass
> of champagne at Christmas,
> but she couldn't resist
> creamy Irish coffee!
> —**REBECCA LITTLE** PARK RIDGE, IL

CARAMEL VANILLA MARTINIS

This rich and delicious martini makes a perfect after-dinner drink for a special dinner. The chocolate swirl inside the glass adds a sophisticated touch.

START TO FINISH: 5 MIN.
MAKES: 2 SERVINGS

Ice cubes
3 ounces amaretto
2 ounces caramel-flavored Irish cream liqueur
1½ teaspoons vanilla vodka
Chocolate syrup, optional

1. Fill a mixing glass or tumbler three-fourths full with ice. Add amaretto, Irish cream liqueur and vodka; stir until condensation forms on outside of glass.
2. Drizzle chocolate syrup on the inside of two chilled cocktail glasses if desired. Strain Amaretto mixture into glasses. Serve immediately.

MULLED GRAPE CIDER

I came up with this recipe one year when my attempt to make grape jelly ended with 30 jars of delicious grape syrup instead. I simmered the syrup with spices to make this pretty autumn drink.

—**SHARON HARMON** ORANGE, MA

PREP: 20 MIN. • **COOK:** 3 HOURS
MAKES: 12 SERVINGS (2¾ QUARTS)

5 pounds Concord grapes
8 cups water, divided
1½ cups sugar
8 whole cloves
4 cinnamon sticks (4 inches)
Dash ground nutmeg

1. In a large saucepan, combine grapes and 2 cups water; bring to a boil, stirring constantly. Press through a strainer; reserve juice and discard skins and seeds.
2. Pour the juice through a double layer of cheesecloth into a 5-qt. slow cooker. Add sugar, cloves, cinnamon sticks, nutmeg and the remaining water. Cover and cook on low for 3 hours. Discard the cloves and cinnamon sticks.

MAKE MINE A *Mocktail*

SPARKLING CELEBRATION PUNCH

Every celebration deserves a gorgeous punch like this one—fruity, bubbly and icy cold. We garnish the punch bowl with slices of oranges, lemons or limes.

—SHARON TIPTON CASSELBERRY, FL

START TO FINISH: 10 MIN.
MAKES: 8 SERVINGS

- ½ to 1 cup brandy
- ½ cup light corn syrup
- 1 bottle (750 milliliters) riesling or other sweet white wine, chilled
- 1 bottle (750 milliliters) champagne, chilled
  Ice cubes
  Orange, lemon or lime slices

In a punch bowl, mix brandy and corn syrup until blended. Stir in riesling; add champagne. Serve over ice with citrus slices.

NOTES

_____
_____
_____
_____
_____
_____
_____
_____

CIDER WASSAIL PUNCH

Cinnamon, cloves, apple cider and cranberry juice blend to create a wonderful drink with an aroma to match. To make this a drink for all ages, delete the rum and add 1 teaspoon of rum extract instead.

—SHARON TIPTON CASSELBERRY, FL

START TO FINISH: 30 MIN.
MAKES: 9 SERVINGS

- 6 **cups apple cider or juice**
- 2 **cups cranberry juice**
- 1 **cup orange juice**
- ¼ **cup sugar**
- 1 **medium orange, quartered**
- 2 **cinnamon sticks (3 inches)**
- 16 **whole cloves**
- 1 **cup rum**
- ½ **teaspoon bitters, optional**
  Orange peel strips, optional

1. In a Dutch oven over medium heat, combine juices and sugar. Place orange, cinnamon sticks and cloves on a double thickness of cheesecloth. Gather corners of cloth to enclose seasonings; tie securely with string. Add spice bag to juices.

2. Bring liquid to a simmer. Add rum and, if desired, bitters and orange slices. Discard spice bag before serving.

HELPFUL HINT

You can also make this drink in a percolator! Put the cider, juices, sugar and bitters in the percolator, the spices and orange slices in the basket. When it's done percolating, add the rum!

BOOZY DESSERTS

AMARETTO CAKE WITH BUTTERCREAM FROSTING

I came up with this recipe because I was craving something that tasted like wedding cake. The texture is similar to pound cake, which is exactly what I wanted. Everyone who tastes it loves it.
—**MEGAN DUDASH** YOUNGSVILLE, NC

PREP: 45 MIN.
BAKE: 30 MIN. + COOLING
MAKES: 16 SERVINGS

- 3½ cups all-purpose flour
- 1 teaspoon baking powder
- ½ cup sour cream
- ½ cup 2% milk
- ½ cup amaretto
- 1 cup butter, softened
- ½ cup shortening
- 3 cups sugar
- 6 large eggs
- 2 teaspoons almond extract
- 1 teaspoon vanilla extract

BUTTERCREAM
- 1⅓ cups butter, softened
- 1 teaspoon vanilla extract
- ½ teaspoon salt
- 7½ to 8 cups confectioners' sugar
- ⅔ cup amaretto
   Optional decorations: toasted sliced almonds, milk chocolate M&M's and melted chocolate

1. Preheat oven to 325°. Line bottoms of three greased 9-in. round baking pans with parchment paper; grease paper.

2. In a bowl, whisk flour and baking powder. In another bowl, whisk sour cream, milk and amaretto until blended. In a large bowl, cream butter, shortening and sugar until light and fluffy. Add the eggs, one at a time, beating well after each addition. Beat in extracts. Add flour mixture alternately with the sour cream mixture, beating well after each addition.

3. Transfer batter to prepared pans. Bake 30-35 minutes or until a toothpick inserted in center comes out clean. Cool in pans 10 minutes before removing to wire racks; remove paper. Cool completely.

4. In a large bowl, beat butter, vanilla and salt until creamy. Beat in enough confectioners' sugar, alternately with amaretto, to reach desired consistency. Reserve ⅔ cup frosting for piping.

5. Place one cake layer on a plate; spread with ½ cup frosting. Top with remaining cake layer. Frost top and sides with remaining frosting.

6. Pipe reserved frosting around bottom edge of cake. If desired, decorate cake with flowers, using almonds for petals and M&M's for the centers. Pipe designs on frosting with melted chocolate as desired.

NOTE *To toast nuts, bake in a shallow pan in a 350° oven for 5-10 minutes or cook in a skillet over low heat until lightly browned, stirring occasionally.*

ORANGE CHOCOLATE RICOTTA PIE

PREP: 20 MIN. • **BAKE:** 40 MIN. + COOLING
MAKES: 8 SERVINGS

- 2 **cartons (15 ounces each) whole-milk ricotta cheese**
- 2 **large eggs, lightly beaten**
- ½ **cup dark chocolate chips**
- ⅓ **cup sugar**
- 1 **tablespoon grated orange peel**
- 2 **tablespoons orange liqueur**
  Refrigerated pastry for double-crust pie (9 inches)

1. Preheat oven to 425°. In a large bowl, combine the ricotta cheese, eggs, chocolate chips, sugar, orange peel and orange liqueur.
2. Roll out half of the pastry to fit a 9-in. pie plate; transfer pastry to pie plate. Fill with ricotta mixture.
3. Roll out remaining pastry into an 11-in. circle; cut into 1-in.-wide strips. Lay half the strips across the pie, about 1-in. apart. Fold back every other strip halfway. Lay another strip across center of pie at a right angle. Unfold strips over center strip. Fold back the alternate strips; place a second strip across the pie. Continue to add strips until pie is covered in a lattice. Trim, seal and flute edges.
4. Bake for 40-45 minutes or until crust is golden brown. Refrigerate leftovers.

A traditional Italian dessert served during the holidays and for special occasions, the orange and chocolate flavors make a classic Italian pairing. The result is rich and tangy—a perfect finale to a Mediterranean-style dinner.

—TRISHA KRUSE EAGLE, ID

RUM RAISIN CREME BRULEE

Inspired by a favorite ice cream flavor, I created this make-ahead recipe to free up some time in the kitchen. You can also serve this as a custard if you choose to not caramelize the top.

—ELEANOR FROEHLICH ROCHESTER, MI

PREP: 20 MIN. • **BAKE:** 30 MIN. + CHILLING
MAKES: 6 SERVINGS

- ⅓ **cup raisins**
- ¼ **cup dark rum**
- 2½ **cups heavy whipping cream**
- 7 **large egg yolks**
- ½ **cup plus 6 teaspoons superfine sugar, divided**

1. Preheat oven to 325°. In a small bowl, toss raisins with rum; microwave for 30 seconds. Let stand 10 minutes.

2. Meanwhile, in a small saucepan, heat cream until bubbles form around the sides of the pan; remove from heat. In a bowl, whisk egg yolks and ½ cup sugar until blended but not foamy. Slowly stir in hot cream. Strain the raisin mixture into the cream mixture, stirring in rum to combine; reserve the raisins.

3. Place six 6-oz. broiler-safe ramekins or custard cups in a baking pan large enough to hold them without touching. Divide the reserved raisins among the ramekins; pour egg mixture over top. Place pan on oven rack; add very hot water to pan to within ¾ in. of top of ramekins.

4. Bake 30-35 minutes or until center is just set and top appears dull. Immediately remove ramekins from water bath to a wire rack; cool 10 minutes. Refrigerate until cold, about 4 hours.

5. Sprinkle custards evenly with remaining sugar. Hold torch flame about 2 in. above custard surface and rotate the ramekin slowly until the sugar is evenly caramelized. Serve immediately or refrigerate up to 1 hour.

IRISH CREAM CUPCAKES

If you're looking for a grown-up cupcake, give these a try. You'll have a hard time limiting yourself to one— good thing they're lighter than some!

—JENNY LEIGHTY WEST SALEM, OH

PREP: 25 MIN. • **BAKE:** 20 MIN. + COOLING
MAKES: 2 DOZEN

- ½ cup butter, softened
- 1½ cups sugar
- 2 large eggs
- ¾ cup unsweetened applesauce
- 2 teaspoons vanilla extract
- 2½ cups all-purpose flour
- 3 teaspoons baking powder
- ½ teaspoon salt
- ½ cup Irish cream liqueur

FROSTING

- ⅓ cup butter, softened
- 4 ounces reduced-fat cream cheese
- 6 tablespoons Irish cream liqueur
- 4 cups confectioners' sugar

1. Preheat oven to 350°. Beat butter and sugar until crumbly, about 2 minutes. Add eggs, one at a time, beating well after each addition. Beat in applesauce and vanilla (mixture may appear curdled). Combine the flour, baking powder and salt; add to the creamed mixture alternately with liqueur, beating well after each addition.

2. Fill paper-lined muffin cups two-thirds full. Bake for 18-22 minutes or until a toothpick inserted in the center comes out clean. Cool for 10 minutes before removing from pans to wire racks to cool completely.

3. For frosting, in a large bowl, beat butter and cream cheese until fluffy. Beat in liqueur. Add confectioners' sugar; beat until smooth. Pipe over tops of cupcakes. Refrigerate leftovers.

CRANBERRY & WALNUT PIE

For a show-stopping holiday pie, I mix cranberries, chocolate and walnuts. A little touch of rum makes it even happier.

—LORRIE MELERINE HOUSTON, TX

PREP: 30 MIN. + CHILLING • **BAKE:** 30 MIN. + COOLING
MAKES: 8 SERVINGS

    Pastry for single-crust pie (9 inches)
3   large eggs
¾   cup sugar
½   cup butter, melted
3   tablespoons all-purpose flour
1   cup chopped walnuts
1   cup fresh or frozen cranberries
1   cup (6 ounces) semisweet chocolate chips
2   tablespoons dark rum

1. On a lightly floured surface, roll the pastry dough to a ⅛-in.-thick circle; transfer to a 9-in. pie plate. Trim pastry to ½ in. beyond rim of plate; flute edge. Refrigerate for 30 minutes. Preheat oven to 450°.

2. Line unpricked pastry with a double thickness of foil. Fill with pie weights, dried beans or uncooked rice. Bake on a lower oven rack 15-20 minutes or until edges are light golden brown. Remove foil and weights; bake 3-6 minutes longer or until bottom is golden brown. Cool on a wire rack. Reduce oven setting to 350°.

3. In a large bowl, beat eggs, sugar and melted butter until well blended. Gradually add flour until blended. Stir in the remaining ingredients; pour into crust.

4. Bake 30-35 minutes or until top is bubbly and crust is golden brown. Cool on a wire rack. Refrigerate leftovers.

NOTE *Pastry for single-crust pie (9 inches): Combine 1¼ cups all-purpose flour and ¼ tsp. salt; cut in ½ cup cold butter until crumbly. Gradually add 3-5 Tbsp. ice water, tossing with a fork until dough holds together when pressed. Wrap in plastic wrap and refrigerate 1 hour.*

GRILLED FIGGY PIES

Delicious figs combined with maple, walnuts and creamy mascarpone make a decadent treat that's easy to enjoy at a backyard cookout. These distinctive hand pies always disappear quickly.
—**RENEE MURBY** JOHNSTON, RI

PREP: 50 MIN. + FREEZING
GRILL: 10 MIN.
MAKES: 1 DOZEN

- 1 **package refrigerated pie pastry**
- 12 **dried figs**
- ¼ **cup bourbon**
- ½ **cup chopped walnuts**
- ¼ **cup plus 1 tablespoon maple syrup, divided**
- 1 **teaspoon ground cinnamon**
- ½ **teaspoon ground nutmeg**
- ½ **teaspoon vanilla extract**
- ⅔ **cup (about 5 ounces) mascarpone cheese**
- 1 **large egg**
- 1 **tablespoon water**

1. Warm the pie pastry to room temperature according to package directions. Meanwhile, in a small saucepan, combine the figs and bourbon; add enough water to cover by 1 in. Cook, covered, over low heat until figs are plump, 15-20 minutes. Remove from heat; drain. Cool for 15 minutes and pat dry. Cut each fig into quarters. Set aside.

2. In the same saucepan over medium-low heat, combine the walnuts with ¼ cup maple syrup, cinnamon and nutmeg. Cook, stirring constantly, until liquid is almost evaporated, 5-7 minutes. Spread nuts on a baking sheet lined with parchment paper; freeze until set, about 10 minutes.

3. Unroll pastry sheets. Using a 4-in. round cutter, cut 12 circles, rolling and cutting the scraps as necessary. Stir vanilla and the remaining maple syrup into the mascarpone cheese. Spread 1 scant tablespoon of the mascarpone mixture over half of each circle to within ¼ in. of edge; layer with 2 teaspoons of the maple walnuts and four fig pieces. Make an egg wash by whisking egg and water; use to moisten edge of pastry. Fold dough over filling; press edges with a fork to seal. Repeat with the remaining dough and filling. Brush egg wash over pies. Freeze pies on a parchment paper-lined baking sheet for 10 minutes.

4. Remove pies from baking sheet. Grill, covered, on a well-greased grill rack over medium direct heat until golden brown, 5-7 minutes per side.

HOLIDAY RUM BALLS

PREP: 30 MIN.
MAKES: ABOUT 2½ DOZEN

- 2 **cups confectioners' sugar**
- ¼ **cup baking cocoa**
- 1 **package (12 ounces) vanilla wafers, finely crushed**
- 1 **cup finely chopped walnuts**
- ½ **cup light corn syrup**
- ¼ **cup rum**
  Additional confectioners' sugar

1. In a large bowl, mix confectioners' sugar and cocoa until blended. Add crushed wafers and walnuts; toss to combine. In another bowl, mix corn syrup and rum; stir into wafer mixture.
2. Shape mixture into 1-in. balls. Roll in additional confectioners' sugar. Store in an airtight container.

> I use this recipe for special occasions with my wonderful family and friends. The sweet cookies are so easy to make and pack a festive rum punch.
>
> —**DIANE DUSCHANEK** COUNCIL BLUFFS, IA

GLAZED SPICED RUM POUND CAKES

My recipe makes two loaf-size treats, perfect for sharing. The spiced rum flavor really comes through in both the cake and the glaze.

—CHRISTINE RUSSELL LITTLETON, NH

PREP: 30 MIN.
BAKE: 45 MIN. + COOLING
MAKES: 2 LOAVES (8 SLICES EACH)

- 1 **cup butter, softened**
- 2 **cups packed brown sugar**
- 5 **large eggs**
- ⅓ **cup spiced rum**
- 2 **teaspoons vanilla extract**
- 3½ **cups all-purpose flour**
- 2 **teaspoons baking powder**
- ½ **teaspoon baking soda**
- ½ **teaspoon salt**
- ½ **cup 2% milk**

GLAZE
- ½ **cup sugar**
- ¼ **cup butter, cubed**
- 2 **teaspoons water**
- 2 **teaspoons spiced rum**
- ½ **cup chopped pecans, toasted**

1. Preheat oven to 350°. Grease and flour two 9x5-in. loaf pans. In a large bowl, cream butter and brown sugar until light and fluffy. Add eggs, one at a time, beating well after each addition. Beat in rum and vanilla. In another bowl, whisk flour, baking powder, baking soda and salt; add to creamed mixture alternately with the milk, beating well after each addition.

2. Spoon batter into the prepared pans. Bake 45-50 minutes or until a toothpick inserted in center comes out clean. Cool in pans 10 minutes before removing to wire racks.

3. Meanwhile, in a small saucepan, combine sugar, butter, water and rum. Bring to a boil. Remove from heat; drizzle glaze over warm cakes. Sprinkle with pecans. Cool cakes completely on wire racks.

NOTE *To toast nuts, bake in a shallow pan in a 350° oven for 5-10 minutes or cook in a skillet over low heat until lightly browned, stirring occasionally.*

MOLASSES-BOURBON PECAN PIE

Guests' mouths water when they glimpse this southern charmer. Its flaky crust perfectly complements the rich, nutty filling.

—CHARLENE CHAMBERS
ORMOND BEACH, FL

PREP: 35 MIN. + CHILLING
BAKE: 55 MIN. + COOLING
MAKES: 8 SERVINGS

- 1½ **cups all-purpose flour**
- ¾ **teaspoon salt**
- 6 **tablespoons shortening**
- 5 **to 6 tablespoons ice water**

FILLING

- ¾ **cup packed brown sugar**
- ¾ **cup corn syrup**
- ½ **cup molasses**
- 3 **tablespoons butter**
- ½ **teaspoon salt**
- 3 **large eggs, beaten**
- 2 **tablespoons bourbon**
- 2 **teaspoons vanilla extract**
- 2 **cups pecan halves**
  Whipped cream

1. In a large bowl, combine flour and salt; cut in shortening until crumbly. Gradually add water, tossing with a fork until dough forms a ball. Wrap in plastic. Refrigerate for 1 to 1½ hours or until easy to handle.

2. Roll out pastry to fit a 9-in. pie plate. Transfer pastry to pie plate. Trim pastry to ½ in. beyond edge of plate; flute edge. Refrigerate.

3. Meanwhile, in a large saucepan, combine brown sugar, corn syrup, molasses, butter and salt; bring to a simmer over medium heat. Cook and stir for 2-3 minutes or until sugar is dissolved. Remove from the heat and cool to room temperature. (Mixture will be thick when cooled.)

4. Preheat oven to 350°. Stir eggs, bourbon and vanilla into molasses mixture. Stir in pecans. Pour into pastry shell. Bake 55-60 minutes or until a knife inserted in the center comes out clean. Cover edges with foil during the last 30 minutes to prevent overbrowning if necessary.

5. Cool on a wire rack. Serve with whipped cream. Refrigerate any leftovers.

SOUTHERN LANE CAKE

I just love this impressive and festive cake—and so do my dinner guests. The fruit filling and topping remind me of a fruit cake, but this version is so much more delicious!

—**MABEL PARVI** RIDGEFIELD, WA

PREP: 40 MIN.
BAKE: 20 MIN. + CHILLING
MAKES: 12 SERVINGS

- 6 **large egg whites**
- ¾ **cup butter, softened**
- 1½ **cups sugar**
- 1 **teaspoon vanilla extract**
- 2¼ **cups all-purpose flour**
- 2½ **teaspoons baking powder**
- ½ **teaspoon salt**
- ¾ **cup 2% milk**

FILLING

- 6 **large egg yolks**
- 1 **cup sugar**
- ½ **cup butter, cubed**
- ¼ **cup bourbon**
- 1 **tablespoon grated orange peel**
- ¼ **teaspoon salt**
- ¾ **cup raisins**
- ¾ **cup sweetened shredded coconut**
- ¾ **cup chopped pecans**
- ¾ **cup coarsely chopped red candied cherries**
- 1 **cup heavy whipping cream, whipped and sweetened**

1. Line bottoms of three greased 9-in. round baking pans with parchment paper; grease paper; set aside. Place egg whites in a large bowl; let stand at room temperature 30 minutes. Preheat oven to 350°.

2. In another large bowl, cream butter and sugar until light and fluffy. Beat in vanilla. In another bowl, whisk flour, baking powder and salt; add to creamed mixture alternately with milk, beating well after each addition. Beat egg whites until stiff peaks form; fold into batter. Transfer to prepared pans.

3. Bake for 20-25 minutes or until a toothpick inserted in the center comes out clean. Cool layers for 10 minutes before removing from pans to wire racks; remove paper. Cool completely.

4. For filling, combine egg yolks and sugar in a large saucepan. Add butter; cook and stir over medium-low heat until sugar is dissolved and mixture thickens (do not boil). Remove from the heat. Stir in the bourbon, orange peel and salt. Fold in raisins, coconut, pecans and cherries. Cool.

5. Place one cake layer on a serving plate; spread with a third of the filling. Repeat layers twice. Frost sides of cake with whipped cream. Refrigerate until serving.

NOTE *Cake can be made and filled a day in advance. Cover, refrigerate; remove from the refrigerator 30 minutes before serving and frost.*

LITTLE AMARETTO LOAF CAKES

Using smaller pans and topping the cakes with amaretto glaze makes these loaves so incredibly moist.

—DONNA LAMANO OLATHE, KS

PREP: 25 MIN.
BAKE: 35 MIN. + STANDING
MAKES: 4 MINI LOAVES (6 SLICES EACH)

- 4 **large eggs**
- 1 **cup sugar**
- ½ **cup water**
- ½ **cup amaretto**
- ½ **cup canola oil**
- ¼ **cup butter, melted**
- 2 **cups all-purpose flour**
- 3 **teaspoons baking powder**
- 1 **teaspoon salt**
- ¾ **cup sliced almonds**

GLAZE
- ½ **cup sugar**
- ½ **cup water**
- ¼ **cup butter, cubed**
- ¼ **cup amaretto**

1. Preheat oven to 325°. Grease and flour four 5¾x3x2-in. loaf pans.

2. In a large bowl, beat eggs, sugar, water, amaretto, oil and melted butter until well blended. In another bowl, whisk flour, baking powder and salt; gradually beat into egg mixture. Stir in almonds.

3. Transfer to prepared pans. Bake 35-40 minutes or until a toothpick inserted in center comes out clean.

4. Meanwhile, for glaze, combine sugar, water and butter in a small saucepan; bring to a boil. Cook and stir 3 minutes. Remove from heat; stir in amaretto.

5. Remove cakes from oven; cool in pans on a wire rack 5 minutes. Pour glaze over cakes while in pans; let stand until glaze is absorbed, about 30 minutes. Remove cakes from pans. Store cooled cakes, covered, in refrigerator.

NOTES

MUDSLIDE CHEESECAKE

I change up my cheesecakes with different liqueur flavorings. This mudslide version with coffee and Irish cream is my husband's favorite.
—**SUE GRONHOLZ** BEAVER DAM, WI

PREP: 30 MIN.
BAKE: 1 HOUR + COOLING
MAKES: 16 SERVINGS

- 1 **cup chocolate wafer crumbs**
- 3 **tablespoons sugar**
- 2 **tablespoons butter, melted**

FILLING

- 1 **cup (6 ounces) semisweet chocolate chips**
- 4 **packages (8 ounces each) cream cheese, softened**
- 1½ **cups sugar**
- 4 **tablespoons all-purpose flour**
- 4 **large eggs, room temperature**
- 2 **teaspoons vanilla extract**
- 2 **tablespoons coffee liqueur**
- ¾ **cup Irish cream liqueur**

GANACHE

- ½ **cup (3 ounces) semisweet chocolate chips**
- ¼ **cup heavy whipping cream**

1. Preheat oven to 325°. Wrap a double thickness of heavy-duty foil (about 18 in. square) around the outside of a greased 9-in. springform pan. Mix cookie crumbs and sugar; stir in butter. Press onto bottom of prepared pan.

2. For filling, microwave chocolate chips on high until melted, about 1 minute. Beat cream cheese and sugar until smooth. Add flour; mix well. Add eggs and vanilla; beat on low just until blended. Measure out 2 cups batter, and stir in coffee liqueur; add melted chocolate chips and stir until blended. Pour over crust. Add Irish cream liqueur to the remaining batter; spoon over chocolate layer. Place springform pan in a larger baking pan; add 1 in. of hot water to the larger pan.

3. Bake until center is just set and the top appears dull, 60-75 minutes. Remove springform pan from water bath and cool on a wire rack for 10 minutes. Loosen sides of cake from pan with a knife; remove foil. Cool 1 hour longer. Refrigerate until completely cooled; cover cake and refrigerate overnight.

4. For ganache, microwave the chocolate chips and whipping cream on high until chips melt; cool slightly. Remove rim from pan; spread ganache on the chilled cheesecake.

HAPPY HOUR
APPETIZERS

SALMON PARTY SPREAD

We're proud to serve our delicious Alaskan salmon to guests. Set out some crackers, and this slightly smoky spread will be gone in no time!

—KATHY CROW CORDOVA, AK

PREP: 10 MIN. + CHILLING
MAKES: 2 CUPS

- 1 **package (8 ounces) cream cheese, softened**
- 1 **can (7½ ounces) pink salmon, drained, flaked and cartilage removed**
- 3 **tablespoons chopped fresh parsley**
- 2 **tablespoons finely chopped green pepper**
- 2 **tablespoons finely chopped sweet red pepper**
- 2 **teaspoon lemon juice**
- 1 **teaspoon prepared horseradish**
- ½ **teaspoon Liquid Smoke, optional**
  Finely chopped pecans or additional parsley
  Crackers

In a bowl, combine the first eight ingredients; stir until well blended. Cover and chill 2-24 hours. Transfer to a serving bowl; sprinkle with pecans or parsley. Serve with crackers.

MARINATED MOZZARELLA

PREP: 15 MIN. + MARINATING
MAKES: 10 SERVINGS

⅓ **cup olive oil**
1 **tablespoon chopped oil-packed sun-dried tomatoes**
1 **tablespoon minced fresh parsley**
1 **teaspoon crushed red pepper flakes**
1 **teaspoon dried basil**
1 **teaspoon minced chives**
¼ **teaspoon garlic powder**
1 **pound cubed part-skim mozzarella cheese**

In a large bowl, combine the first seven ingredients; add the cheese cubes. Stir to coat. Cover; refrigerate for at least 30 minutes.

I always come home with an empty container when I bring this dish to a party. It can be made ahead to free up time later. I serve it with pretty party picks for a festive look.

—**PEGGY CAIRO** KENOSHA, WI

EASY BUFFALO CHICKEN DIP

Folks will simply devour this savory and delicious dip, packed with shredded chicken. The spicy kick makes it perfect football-watching food, and the recipe always brings raves.

—**JANICE FOLTZ** HERSHEY, PA

START TO FINISH: 30 MIN.
MAKES: 4 CUPS

- 1 **package (8 ounces) reduced-fat cream cheese**
- 1 **cup reduced-fat sour cream**
- ½ **cup Louisiana-style hot sauce**
- 3 **cups shredded cooked chicken breast**
  Assorted crackers

1. Preheat oven to 350°. In a large bowl, beat cream cheese, sour cream and hot sauce until smooth; stir in chicken.
2. Transfer to an 8-in. square baking dish coated with cooking spray. Cover and bake 18-22 minutes or until heated through. Serve warm with crackers.

MARMALADE MEATBALLS

I brought this snappy recipe to work for a potluck. I started the meatballs in the slow cooker in the morning, and by lunchtime they were ready.
—**JEANNE KISS** GREENSBURG, PA

PREP: 10 MIN. • **COOK:** 4 HOURS
MAKES: ABOUT 5 DOZEN

- 1 **bottle (16 ounces) Catalina salad dressing**
- 1 **cup orange marmalade**
- 3 **tablespoons Worcestershire sauce**
- ½ **teaspoon crushed red pepper flakes**
- 1 **package (32 ounces) frozen fully cooked home-style meatballs, thawed**

In a 3-qt. slow cooker, combine the salad dressing, marmalade, Worcestershire sauce and pepper flakes. Stir in meatballs. Cover and cook on low for 4-5 hours or until heated through.

FREEZE OPTION *Freeze cooled meatball mixture in freezer containers. To use, partially thaw in refrigerator overnight. Microwave, covered, on high in a microwave-safe dish until heated through, gently stirring and adding a little water if necessary.*

EASY PARTY MEATBALLS *Omit first four ingredients. Combine 1 bottle (14 ounces) ketchup, ¼ cup A.1. steak sauce, 1 tablespoon minced garlic and 1 teaspoon Dijon mustard in slow cooker; stir in meatballs. Cook as directed.*

TOASTED RAVIOLI PUFFS

I call toasted ravioli a fan favorite— because it disappears faster than I can make it. With just five ingredients, this is how you start the party.
—**KATHY MORGAN** TEMECULA, CA

START TO FINISH: 30 MIN.
MAKES: 2 DOZEN

- 24 **refrigerated cheese ravioli**
- 1 **tablespoon reduced-fat Italian salad dressing**
- 1 **tablespoon Italian-style panko (Japanese) bread crumbs**
- 1 **tablespoon grated Parmesan cheese**
  Warm marinara sauce

1. Preheat oven to 400°. Cook ravioli according to the package directions; drain. Transfer to a greased baking sheet. Brush with salad dressing. In a small bowl, mix bread crumbs and cheese; sprinkle over ravioli.

2. Bake 12-15 minutes or until golden brown. Serve ravioli with marinara sauce.

HELPFUL HINT

Nonstick pans still need a bit of grease. Start by rubbing a small amount of oil or butter on your pan. Don't use cooking sprays; those usually have additives that might damage the nonstick coating.

SAVORY PARTY BREAD

It's impossible to stop nibbling on this warm, cheesy, oniony loaf. The bread fans out for a fun presentation.

—KAY DALY RALEIGH, NC

PREP: 10 MIN. • **BAKE:** 25 MIN.
MAKES: 8 SERVINGS

- **1 unsliced round loaf sourdough bread (1 pound)**
- **1 pound Monterey Jack cheese**
- **½ cup butter, melted**
- **½ cup chopped green onions**
- **2 to 3 teaspoons poppy seeds**

1. Preheat oven to 350°. Cut bread widthwise into 1-in. slices to within ½ in. of bottom of loaf. Repeat cuts in opposite direction. Cut cheese into ¼-in. slices; cut slices into small pieces. Place cheese in cuts.

2. In a small bowl, mix butter, green onions and poppy seeds; drizzle over bread. Wrap in foil; place on a baking sheet. Bake 15 minutes. Unwrap; bake 10 minutes longer or until cheese is melted.

NOTE *The bread can be sliced and filled with cheese a day ahead. Right before company comes, melt the butter and add the green onions and poppy seeds.*

NOTES

_____

_____

_____

_____

_____

_____

_____

TEXAS SALSA

Even after 20 years in Texas, I still can't get enough of our wonderful local citrus. This is one way to work it into a main dish. The combination of tangy fruit, spicy jalapeno and distinctive cilantro is perfect over any meat, poultry or fish. We also dip into it with chips.
—LOIS KILDAHL MCALLEN, TX

PREP: 15 MIN. + CHILLING
MAKES: 12 SERVINGS (⅓ CUP EACH)

- 1 medium green pepper, chopped
- 1 medium sweet red pepper, chopped
- 1 medium sweet yellow pepper, chopped
- 1 medium tomato, seeded and chopped
- 1 jalapeno pepper, seeded and chopped
- 3 tablespoons chopped red onion
- 1 tablespoon minced fresh cilantro
- 1½ teaspoons sugar
- ½ teaspoon salt
- 1 medium red grapefruit
- 1 large navel orange

1. In a large bowl, combine the first nine ingredients.
2. Cut a thin slice off the top and bottom of grapefruit and orange; stand upright on a cutting board. With a knife, cut off peel and outer membrane of fruit. Cut along the membrane of each segment to remove fruit; add fruit to the pepper mixture.
3. Stir gently to combine. Refrigerate, covered, at least 2 hours.

NOTE *Wear disposable gloves when cutting hot peppers; the oils can burn skin. Avoid touching your face.*

CAPRESE SALAD KABOBS

Trade in the usual veggie party platter for these pretty kabobs. I often make them for my family to snack on, and it's a great recipe for the kids to help with.
—**CHRISTINE MITCHELL** GLENDORA, CA

START TO FINISH: 10 MIN.
MAKES: 12 KABOBS

- 24 **grape tomatoes**
- 12 **cherry-size fresh mozzarella cheese balls**
- 24 **fresh basil leaves**
- 2 **tablespoons olive oil**
- 2 **teaspoons balsamic vinegar**

On each of 12 appetizer skewers, thread two tomatoes, one cheese ball and two basil leaves, alternating the ingredients. To serve, whisk together oil and vinegar; drizzle over kabobs.

HELPFUL HINT

When using balsamic vinegar for drizzling (instead of cooking), it's worth splurging on a high-quality brand. If you don't like the dark color, opt for white balsamic instead.

WARM GOAT CHEESE IN MARINARA

Every family has a recipe they pull out time and again when the gang gathers, and goat cheese warmed in a marinara sauce is one of those household favorites. Minced basil and cracked black pepper give it a lively finish.
—**JAN VALDEZ** CHICAGO, IL

START TO FINISH: 30 MIN.
MAKES: 1½ CUPS

- 1 **log (4 ounces) goat cheese**
- 1 **cup marinara or spaghetti sauce**
- 2 **tablespoons minced fresh basil**
- ¼ **teaspoon cracked black pepper**
  Toasted French bread baguette slices or assorted crackers

1. Freeze cheese for 15 minutes. Unwrap and cut into ½-in. slices. In an ungreased small shallow baking dish, combine marinara sauce and basil. Top with cheese slices; sprinkle with pepper.
2. Bake, uncovered, at 350° for 8-10 minutes or until heated through. Serve warm with toasted baguette slices.

ASPARAGUS WITH HORSERADISH DIP

START TO FINISH: 15 MIN.
MAKES: 16 APPETIZERS

32 fresh asparagus spears (about 2 pounds), trimmed
1 cup reduced-fat mayonnaise
¼ cup grated Parmesan cheese
1 tablespoon prepared horseradish
½ teaspoon Worcestershire sauce

1. Place asparagus in a steamer basket; place in a large saucepan over 1 in. of water. Bring to a boil; cover and steam for 2-4 minutes or until crisp-tender. Drain and immediately place in ice water. Drain and pat dry.
2. In a small bowl, combine the remaining ingredients. Serve with asparagus.

This is a terrific dip for party season.
Serve asparagus on a decorative platter
with lemon wedges on the side for garnish.
For a flavor variation, use chopped
garlic in place of the horseradish.

—LYNN CARUSO GILROY, CA

HELPFUL HINT

As an alternative to the whole olives, try chopping them up. The result is something like a warm tapenade instead of olives in sauce. Both ways are delicious!

LEMON-HERB OLIVES WITH GOAT CHEESE

Greek olives have a fruity flavor that comes into play when you mix them with lemon and fresh herbs. Spoon over goat cheese and tuck in crackers.

—JEANNE AMBROSE MILWAUKEE, WI

START TO FINISH: 15 MIN.
MAKES: 6 SERVINGS

- 3 **tablespoons olive oil**
- 2 **teaspoons grated lemon peel**
- 1 **garlic clove, minced**
- ½ **teaspoon minced fresh oregano or rosemary**
- ¼ **teaspoon crushed red pepper flakes**
- ½ **cup assorted pitted Greek olives**
- 1 **package (5.3 ounces) fresh goat cheese**
- 1 **tablespoon minced fresh basil Assorted crackers**

1. In a small skillet, combine the first five ingredients; heat over medium heat 2-3 minutes or just until fragrant, stirring occasionally. Stir in olives; heat through, allowing flavors to blend. Cool mixture completely.

2. To serve, place cheese on a serving plate. Stir basil into olive mixture; spoon over cheese. Serve with crackers.

SLOW COOKER HOT CRAB DIP

One batch of this appetizer isn't enough for my big family, so I often double the recipe. Bits of sweet onion give the creamy dip some crunch.
—**TERRI PERRIER** SIMONTON, TX

PREP: 10 MIN. • **COOK:** 2 HOURS
MAKES: 2 CUPS

- 1 package (8 ounces) cream cheese, softened
- ½ cup finely chopped sweet onion
- ¼ cup grated Parmesan cheese
- ¼ cup mayonnaise
- 2 garlic cloves, minced
- 2 teaspoons sugar
- 1 can (6 ounces) crabmeat, drained, flaked and cartilage removed
  Thinly sliced green onions, optional
  Assorted crackers

In a 1½-qt. slow cooker, combine the first six ingredients; stir in crab. Cover and cook on low for 2-3 hours or until heated through. If desired, sprinkle with green onions. Serve with crackers.

NOTE *To make this recipe in the oven, spread crab mixture into an ungreased 9-in. pie plate. Bake, uncovered, at 375° for 15-20 minutes or until heated through.*

SPICY SHRIMP SALSA

Radishes add a wonderful crunch to this colorful salsa that is also great over grilled fish. There's just enough jalapeno to give flavor without too much of the heat.
—**MARY RELYEA** CANASTOTA, NY

START TO FINISH: 15 MIN.
MAKES: 2 CUPS

- ½ pound cooked shrimp, peeled, deveined and chopped
- 1 large tomato, chopped
- ¼ cup finely chopped onion
- 3 radishes, chopped
- ¼ cup minced fresh cilantro
- 2 tablespoons lime juice
- 1½ teaspoons finely chopped seeded jalapeno pepper
- ¼ teaspoon salt
  Baked tortilla chip scoops

In a small bowl, combine the first eight ingredients. Refrigerate until serving. Serve with chips.

NOTE *Wear disposable gloves when cutting hot peppers; the oils can burn skin. Avoid touching your face.*

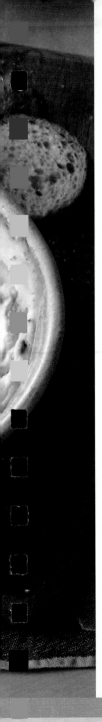

WARM FETA CHEESE DIP

We're huge fans of appetizers, and this super easy baked dip is a mashup of some of our favorite ingredients. It goes so well with a basket of crunchy tortilla chips or slices of a French bread baguette.

—ASHLEY LECKER GREEN BAY, WI

START TO FINISH: 30 MIN.
MAKES: 2 CUPS

- 1 **package (8 ounces) cream cheese, softened**
- 1½ **cups crumbled feta cheese**
- ½ **cup chopped roasted sweet red peppers**
- 3 **tablespoons minced fresh basil or**
  2 teaspoons dried basil
  Sliced French bread baguette or tortilla chips

Preheat oven to 400°. In a small bowl, beat cream cheese, feta cheese, peppers and basil until blended. Transfer to a greased 3-cup baking dish. Bake 25-30 minutes or until bubbly. Serve with baguette slices or chips.

NOTE *To prepare in a slow cooker, mix ingredients as directed. Pour into a greased 1½-qt. slow cooker; cook, covered, on low for 2-3 hours or until heated through.*

NOTES

INDEX